FACING THE JAGUAR

A Memoir of Courage and Confrontation

Babs Walters

Copyright © 2025 Babs Walters

All rights reserved. No part of this publication may be reproduced, distributed, or transmitted in any form or by any means, including photocopying, recording, digital scanning, or other electronic or mechanical methods, without the prior written permission of the publisher, except in the case of brief quotations embodied in critical reviews and certain other noncommercial uses permitted by copyright law. For permission requests, please address She Writes Press.

Published 2025
Printed in the United States of America
Print ISBN: 978-1-64742-920-1
E-ISBN: 978-1-64742-921-8
Library of Congress Control Number: 2025900997

For information, address:
She Writes Press
1569 Solano Ave #546
Berkeley, CA 94707

Interior Design by Kiran Spees
She Writes Press is a division of SparkPoint Studio, LLC.

Company and/or product names that are trade names, logos, trademarks, and/or registered trademarks of third parties are the property of their respective owners and are used in this book for purposes of identification and information only under the Fair Use Doctrine.

NO AI TRAINING: Without in any way limiting the author's [and publisher's] exclusive rights under copyright, any use of this publication to "train" generative artificial intelligence (AI) technologies to generate text is expressly prohibited. The author reserves all rights to license uses of this work for generative AI training and development of machine learning language models.

Names and identifying characteristics have been changed to protect the privacy of certain individuals.

Praise for *Facing the Jaguar*

"Facing the Jaguar is one of the few books that will hold you spellbound from the very first page till the last. . . . Babs Walters is a beautiful writer, and I look forward to reading more of her work. I also applaud her bravery, courage, and strength in sharing her story."

—*Readers' Favorite*, **5-star review**

"Facing the Jaguar is a powerful story of reclamation. Walters's evocative and honest writing takes readers through experiences of childhood abuse, dissociation, and conflicting emotions. Without offering advice or excuses, she reveals what it takes to heal. This is a must-read for anyone seeking to understand a survivor's journey or for survivors looking for healing and hope."

—**Jane Epstein, survivor, TEDx speaker, cofounder of 5WAVES.org,
and author of *I Feel Real Guilty***

"In this honest and raw memoir, Walters exposes a secret that burdens the souls of countless children—because most don't tell. Her story is a plea to all adults to believe and help the courageous children who do tell. An important and brave journey from a frightened child to an empowered woman."

—**Feather Berkower, MSW, author of *Off Limits:
A Parent's Guide to Keeping Kids Safe from Sexual Abuse***

"In her gritty and authentic memoir, Babs Walters courageously reveals the secret life she lived as an abused child and young adult—and how she coped. Her poetic and powerful writing reveals the mark that trauma leaves and how Babs learned to hide to protect herself. Babs used her bright and creative mind to heal and ultimately to become a voice for others who have suffered such traumas. This is a touching and emotionally resonant book for every child who has to grow up without the love and support they need. A must-read!"

—**Linda Joy Myers, president of the National Association of Memoir Writers
and author of *Don't Call Me Mother* and *Song of the Plains***

"Initially nervous I might need to read this memoir much like I would watch a troubling film—through my fingers and ready to look away in an instant—I quickly realized this poignant book, told so clearly and with the most stunning of prose, deserved my complete attention. *Facing the Jaguar* is a chilling, honest account of parental abuse, but it is also a story of hope, tenacity, and the belief that with hard work and a determination to understand, the cycle of generational trauma can be terminated."

—**Patti Eddington, author of *The Girl with Three Birthdays: An Adopted
Daughter's Memoir of Tiaras, Tough Truths, and Tall Tales***

"Babs Walters recounts her life with a poignant and introspective perspective, asserting that she is neither the victim nor the heroine but merely the teller of her story. Through vivid imagery, she describes her life and captures the long-lasting impact of trauma and survival. Ultimately, this memoir is a testament to her quiet resilience and ability to HUSH No More that will encourage other survivors to do the same."

—**Dr. Vanessa Dunn Guyton, survivor advocate and executive director of HUSH No More**

"A public advocate for childhood sexual abuse survivors who has developed workshops for women dealing with abuse, addiction, and domestic violence, Walters tells her story not just for personal catharsis but also to provide inspiration to survivors, demonstrating that courage, personal autonomy, and healing are possible. The book's lean, focused text does not leave room for tangential stories, underscoring its fierce insistence that confronting abuse head-on is an essential step on the path to recovery. A painful but powerful story of abuse and the long road to healing."

—*Kirkus Reviews*

"In *Facing the Jaguar*, Walters takes us on a personal journey, challenging the stigma of childhood abuse and poverty and overcoming the shame of the unspoken—incest. This is a story that will tear at your heart for the little girl, then have you wildly applauding the courageous woman she becomes."

—**Jean Kraljev, LMHC**

"*Facing the Jaguar* is a small book with a huge impact. Despite the abuse of her childhood and young-adult life, Walters comes of age turning these experiences around to survive and begin healing. Her words inspire others to confront their own family secrets, their own jaguars. This is a true story of a brave woman giving meaning and purpose to uncontrollable circumstances."

—**Randi Busse, author of *Turning Rants into Raves***

"In this profoundly moving memoir, Babs Walters demonstrates extraordinary bravery and resilience by sharing her harrowing experiences with family secrets of domestic violence and child sexual abuse. The decision to bring these deeply personal and painful truths into the light is not only an act of remarkable courage but also a gift to others who have faced similar struggles."

—**Jeniffer Thompson, host of *The Premise* podcast**

This book is dedicated to all my sisters
who were obedient and loyal to their families,
who kept the secrets they were told not to share,
who could not find someone to listen
or someone who could hear them,
who held the pain inside themselves for far too long,
who felt all alone.
Here's to all the family secret-keepers.
Here's to telling.

Trigger Warning: This memoir contains references to domestic violence and childhood sexual abuse that may be disturbing or triggering to some readers.

This is a true story of my lived experience and memory. To protect the privacy of the individuals involved, many of the names have been changed.

Prologue

I make the decision. This time I am going to tell him that the relationship is over. No beating around the bush or room for misinterpretation. Crystal clear language in the simplest of terms.

Unlike my other visits with him since my mother died, I am not bringing my father a cooked meal or fresh vegetables from the farmer's market to tide him over for a few days. No gifts or offerings of any kind. No phone numbers for contacting Meals on Wheels. No help with packing up unused clothes to empty Mom's closet. Or cleaning bookshelves crammed with a lifetime of photo albums and musty old paperbacks, or the garage filled with remnants of car and machine parts, or the guest bedroom stuffed with one-of-a-kind oddities like a spare closet. I am on a mission. One that's entirely on my own terms.

I write down the words I plan to say and practice them several times. I anticipate what can go wrong. Nothing, I conclude. I am going to his house and can walk out anytime I want. He is no longer physically well enough to follow or chase me. What I dread most is the invisible, electrically charged current I always experience that radiates from his body and crawls over my skin anytime I get too close to him. The experience is not unlike getting too close to the flames of a blazing fire where the more heat you feel, the more your body is forced back. His proximity has always provoked profound stress.

I arrive empty-handed and don't even want to sit down. He is in the kitchen, one of the few places left uncluttered in the house. The dining and living rooms are now being used for storage of about a dozen boxes with medical records. He plans to read them all and sue the hospitals and doctors for malpractice in their treatment of my mother years earlier. The dining room table is stacked with insurance and police record folders from his two car accidents this past year, of which he believes he was wrongfully accused and they are someone else's fault.

He doesn't get up when I walk in, and I want to be able to look directly into his eyes. So, I sit down across from him on the only other chair not covered in mail. Before I can even start to speak, he tells me about problems he is having. I understand that people who live alone long for someone to witness their daily trials. I notice that I am making excuses for him and will myself to stop.

"The medical alert company is a rip-off," he starts. "They just raised the monthly cost for something I don't ever plan on using. Don't they know that I am on a fixed income? They don't really care about seniors like me. I have plenty of other watches and will wear one of them from now on. I'll show them." He smiles a sly grin as though he is victorious.

The medical alert watch is for his own good, but I swallow my warning.

"Dad," I jump in before he begins his usual riff.

But he out-shouts me. A typical move. He has had another car accident. Of course, it is the other three cars' fault. The crooked cops, too. He was taken to the hospital when the police report was filled out. So, no wonder the bastards all took that opportunity to put the blame on him.

Of course, he complains about how his three children are so busy that they can't take care of him. Can't do the things for him he is having difficulty doing since the accident. Since Mom died. Especially me, who lives so close. Who should know better. He needs someone to fight with the police, the insurance company, the car rental place. Take up his mission with my mother's medical records.

Even if he says nothing else, I can tell he wants me to do something for him that I won't want to do, that he has no right to expect. I feel shaky but confident with what I'm about to do. I need to interrupt his rant.

But how do I capture a lifetime of hurt? Of pain? Of struggle? Of continued abuse? Now that he's in pain and wants my help, no wonder I feel sick inside. I am fighting with myself about whether I should or should not help. Why should he get what he needs? What about all those years and what I needed? This is all a one-way relationship. Or is it?

After all, he gave his sperm. He sacrificed, too, with years of working to keep a roof over our heads. But then there were his life lessons—children should be seen and not heard, don't make waves, I'm doing this for your own good so you won't be frigid like your mother, you can never tell anyone or I'll have to kill you, or go to jail, etc.

What do I owe him, really? I didn't ask for any of it—the good or the bad.

"Dad," I say a little too loudly, staring right into his eyes. "I've made a decision." I hear my voice shaking a little. But he is hard of hearing and probably doesn't notice.

I take a deeper than usual inhalation and plunge. "I have something to tell you. So please listen," I continue. "I feel that I have given you more than I wanted to in my lifetime. That you have taken more from me than anyone should ever expect." I notice the cadence of my voice, so much like his when he races and runs on when he doesn't want anyone else to break in. I don't want to be like him, of all people, so I pause but hold up my hand. I see that he sees me, and he doesn't try to interject.

"This is important to me," I say, speaking a little slower so I can watch the reaction on his face. His expression is like stone. Unreadable. "You took a large portion of my childhood and used it for your own needs." I see his mouth begin to move and I hold up my palm again.

"Almost all of my adulthood has been affected by a stolen childhood and your unhealthy behavior toward me."

He doesn't try to speak now, so I keep going. "You have no right to expect me to take care of you or your needs. I spent my entire childhood satisfying your selfish needs at the cost of not discovering or fulfilling my own. You think because the things you did to us are not happening anymore and it's over for you, that it is over for us. You're wrong. Because I was groomed to think I didn't deserve any better, I confused love with sacrifice. I have spent years in therapy. Ruined two marriages. I've made tons of mistakes working out who I am, and how I want to be without your input. I've already given all a human being should have to give to another. More than any child owes a parent. You're on your own."

When I stand up, I'm shaking. When I walk out, I am still shaking. In spite of the exhilaration that comes from saying these words I'd held in for a lifetime, I also feel something else. I feel sad that our story has to end this way. That I can't show my father that I also love him without him taking advantage of that.

Introduction

I am neither the victim nor the heroine of this story. I am merely the teller. The events that happened have been seeping out of me over the past seven decades, like water in a tea kettle that begins with a soft hiss as it slowly boils, then rapidly increases in intense bubbles until the low whistle erupts into a scream.

I have this recurring dream throughout my adult life that started in my childhood.

The sun is so high in the sky that it is blinding. Everything around me looks whitewashed and hazy. The ground I am standing on is light beige, the color of sand on a hot beach day. The pallid high cement wall behind us blends into the ground. The air almost seems electric as it makes rippled lines that zigzag and crackle. I struggle to keep my eyes open.

The line of men in front of me are wearing camouflage uniforms in faded khaki.

My mother, my little sister, and I stand huddled before them when the commander calls them to attention.

"Ready," he shouts.

The soldiers raise their weapons.

"Set," he continues.

We can hear the sound of metal catches being released in unison.

Before he can complete his mission, my mother forcefully pushes my sister and me forward. Then quickly crouches down on the ground behind us.

"Fire!"

Chapter 1

There have been many places where the road I traveled turned unexpectedly, like a switchback turn on a hiking trail, getting steeper while changing directions with no way to see where it will end or what's around the bend. Some of these changes moved me forward, eventually. Quite a few of the paths I followed ended up more like a Halloween corn maze, with me finding myself back in the same place all over again. Coming to a dead end I would give in, retracing my steps or needing to stand in place and catch my breath before venturing out again.

Some of the turns proved positive with me making progress, breaking through toward my inner growth and healing. Others were more like a gradual breaking down in both my physical and mental health. Although, I couldn't have told you that at the time. It's only been upon reflection that I can see the whole map of my life. And which direction was which.

It is 1974 and Richard Nixon resigns after the Watergate scandal. It is a big year for him and a big year for me. It is also the year my second child has finally begun to sleep through the night. I don't know how I survived with just a couple of hours of sleep each night for two entire years. It is not her fault. She has an immature digestive system and needs to feed and eliminate every few hours. I manage to get by on lots of coffee and even more cigarettes all day. I am not complaining. Just tired.

We have new social demands, all of a sudden. My husband Garry and I join a bowling league and make new friends. People seem to enjoy having me on their team since I am not well coordinated and get the highest handicap in the league. This results in extra bonus points for whichever team I am on. The group has a second dividing line besides high and low bowling averages. There are the wilder couples, beer drinking, tight-jean wearing with frayed bell-bottoms, teased hair for women or slicked back for guys, drawing even more attention to themselves by laughing overly loud, continuing at an afterparty. Then there is the dowdy mommy and daddy homebody crew, wearing tie-dyed T-shirts with at least one spit-up stain somewhere on them and who rush home after play to relieve their sitters. Surprisingly, we are invited to the first group's parties where couples dance and drink and get high. Because I think these women are prettier, have more freedom, and know how to have fun, I push Garry to participate. Life is difficult enough. These people make it look easy. I want to be swept along in their ease, to be liked, to fit in. So I go along with it all.

No sleep, no food, and loose boundaries all begin to build up, weakening my ability to think clearly. I can't fully explain it, but I am drawn to this group of people. Garry would prefer just staying home, playing with the new Pachinko machine he bought or going to sleep early. I am a burden to him. He has said those words often. None of the other husbands we know have to deal with wives who have a family like mine, a history like mine. While I feel sorry for challenging his ability to understand or support me, I also want to belong to the in-crowd.

When I get a call out of the blue from one of the other husbands, I am both surprised and excited. My heart noticeably starts racing in my chest. It's a good thing he can't see me through the landline.

"I'd like to get together sometime, just the two of us," he starts. "You're not like the other women and I'd . . ." He hesitates. "I'd like to get to know you better."

I feel uncomfortable, never having received an invitation like this before. He wants to get together just with me, not Garry. This doesn't feel quite right. But I want more of feeling new and not a burden. I want to see me through his eyes. So I agree.

When you come across an accumulation of large boulders on the trail, it's time to lower your center of gravity and scramble, literally crawl over or around them. That's how I approached the first meeting with my father the same year. I sunk to my belly about as low as I could get.

The day we get together, my father, my sister, and me, it's as if my mind leaves the room. Only my body slowly walks forward. The room is dark. My head is pounding in sync with my accelerating heart, so off pace with my slow movements. I feel myself start to shake like my insides will rebel and take flight following my sense of reason. *Why am I here?*

I fear for my life. Yet I came voluntarily. Well, not exactly. I am here out of guilt. I owe my sister this one last request at least. I am the responsible older one. Aren't big sisters supposed to protect their younger ones? Besides, my sister is relentless.

I am twenty-nine years old, and while I would not have chosen this meeting, I would like some answers. I have had many questions over the years, especially: Why? At the same time I wonder if I will be alive after this, in which case the opportunity to reflect back on whatever answers I might hear will be a lost cause.

I sit down on one of the hard wooden chairs, knowing I am present and absent at the same time. It all feels surreal. This is not how I spend my days. I am a suburban housewife and a stay-at-home mom with a young son and a younger daughter. I cook. I clean. Changing nasty diapers is as scary as it gets. I feel safe in that role and focus on keeping my family safe too.

Willing myself back in the room, I notice a small window that I try to look out of to get perspective. My sister called for a six o'clock meeting after work. As the minutes tick by, and nighttime arrives, the outside provides less and less light. We are here with our father. It seems a fitting backdrop for waking up in a nightmare. I sit leaning left toward my sister, slouching deeply into my seat, as though the weight of me pressing down will prevent me from evaporating in fright. I become the buffer between my father and my sister, a role I never considered when we were younger. The reason I feel guilty today.

Even though the three of us are sitting so closely at the small table, I feel all alone in the universe. Like once more in my life, there is no protection to be had. A feeling I had not had since leaving home nine years earlier. My sister's husband stands at the ready outside the room behind the closed door. My husband remains at home, having opted not to participate. This is my sister's apartment, and she at least has me and her husband in her corner. I feel invisible.

He said he would kill us, this angry but proud gun collector who becomes even more violent after consuming alcohol. He is one of the adults in the role of would-be caretaker who was supposed to be our protector. *How does a bullet feel when it enters your body? Will I die immediately or suffer for a long time in pain?* I force myself to stop thinking like this. *Who will take care of my children if I don't come home? Can a person die from their own fearful thoughts?*

I had erected such a thick protective barrier around myself, a callous born of pain and continued overuse that only now that I'm here do I feel the real danger I had put myself in.

I am not ready for my young life to be over. Yet I put myself into this perilous moment, free-falling from dangerous heights without a parachute or net beneath me. I don't want to die. I have a lot to live for.

Well, my life almost ended once already this year. Remembering the smell of the gas as it filled my lungs and my conscious thoughts being washed away lulls me again when I notice someone has started speaking.

That same year, I also venture out on my first solo adult activity—tennis. The indoor tennis center not only offers year-round play regardless of weather but complimentary childcare. The fact that I am clumsy doesn't stop me from cautiously signing up for a women's beginners' league. We play doubles so my partners end up covering the court, doing the work that requires coordination.

I am over budget with the tennis membership fee and cannot afford lessons, which I sorely need. Feeling embarrassed by how many times I miss the ball, even when it comes right to me, I eagerly sign up for a free class called "The Psychological Game of Tennis." I have been a process observer ever since I can remember, learning the nuances of people's behavior and moods. So this is what I think I might be better at than connecting with the ball. Or if not, I can learn something to help me minimize my negative self-talk on the court.

All together we are about ten women sitting in a semicircle on upholstered couches waiting for the lesson to begin. Carolynn, the counselor giving the class, says she is going to hypnotize us. It has only been a few days since my two-year-old has begun to sleep through the night and I feel drowsy even before we are instructed to close our eyes. I don't remember anything about the brief guided meditation until we are told to open our eyes. Everyone is silently looking at me. Of the group, I am the only one apparently who was hypnotized. I feel silly, like the other women are laughing at me. Remembering comedy skits from TV hypnotists, I wonder what I said or did while under.

Seeing my discomfort, the counselor stays after to chat with me.

"I've never been hypnotized before," I explain, always ready with an apology.

Carolynn smiles and says, "Well I'm glad you were open to the possibility."

"But no one else was. That makes me sort of weird. Doesn't it?"

"No," she smiles again and pauses. "That makes you vulnerable and willing. That's all. The others were uptight." Letting that sink in, Carolynn pauses once more, then asks a non-tennis-related question. "What's going on in your life right now anyway?"

The feeling like I am going to cry in front of a total stranger, even though she is a therapist, causes the muscles around my mouth and eyes to freeze, stopping me from immediately sharing. Instead, my body communicates what I am feeling. My eyes sting and burn with the effort of holding back tears ready to spill. And I can feel blotches of heat and embarrassment becoming visible on my cheeks.

I had buried the past for so long that I feared it rising to the surface and having to feel it again. I was terrified that it would leave me depleted and empty. The protective shield I constructed allowed me to live my life like nothing was wrong or different. I lived in a bubble with *Happy Days* on the outside and *The Exorcist* on the inside. Bursting this bubble, like a giant blister, would leave me raw and bloody, sensitive to the lightest touch.

As long as I could remember, I spent my life looking for answers, or even a tow rope. Here were three occasions where I was going to be exposed. The extramarital affair. The confrontation with my father. A new therapist friend. Who would I find underneath all this coverup? Who would I be without my façade? And who can I trust to help me across the ravine?

If I am going to make it, my first step will be to quiet the words of my father: "Children should be seen and not heard. Don't make waves. We don't talk about things that go on in the family. Or I'll have to kill you."

Chapter 2

"Let's go, Barbara," my mother says with a wave of her arm, making a wide swoop and circling back, meaning I should hurry up and follow her. We are leaving our apartment on Willis Avenue in the Bronx. It's a railroad flat with three rooms that require walking through each one in order to enter the others and a communal bathroom on the second-floor landing.

I am five years old, and we walk together in silence the three blocks from our tenement apartment toward a one-story brick building I have never seen before. My mother takes my hand as we cross each street then lets it go once we step up on a sidewalk again. We climb several cement steps and enter the first door we come to into a dimly lit and empty hallway. I can hear our shoes clicking noisily in unison on the square tiles, which are black and white like a big game board. We walk toward a second door. We both stand facing it for a moment when my mother opens the door and prods me from behind into a room, closing it between us. I wonder what to do or where I am.

In my confusion, I feel my body grow stiff as though my legs are weighted down, glued by the soles of my shoes to the floor. There are children everywhere. Some are standing and talking. Some are sitting at little tables all lined up in rows. The woman in the front of the room points with her outstretched arm and directs me toward the closet in the rear.

"Find a hook and hang up your sweater, dear," she says.

Not knowing where to keep my gaze, I walk to the back of the room, casting my eyes downward, sneaking glances by only moving

13

my eyes to the side. That's when I notice that the other girls I pass wear white socks that fold over at their ankles, several with ruffles. My socks are brown and the stretched-out backs of them seem to slip further down into my shoes with each step, baring my heels. The other girls wear light-colored frilly dresses with lacey underskirts showing at their hem edges. I have never seen anything like this before. My plaid dress is wrinkled and clings down to my sides in folds. The other girls have curls and ribbons and shiny clean hair. Even the boys have trim, patted down hair. My hair feels sticky and lays in separate clumps against my head. And then there is my sweater that the woman called attention to. Although it had been handmade for me, it is old and a little too small and filled with bumpy nubs, dangling like fringe all over.

When I step up into the closet, all the front hooks are already taken. I walk slowly into the right side of the closet looking for an empty hook. Just then, the woman in the front of the room asks a boy sitting in the back to close the closet doors. I think she must not notice that I am still inside. In the next moment, I realize that I can call out but choose not to. I am afraid and embarrassed to draw any more attention to my late arrival and sorry appearance.

I don't know how long I remain in the closet. I sit on the floor and watch the room through a mesh grate I find near the bottom at one side. As I sit there, I grow angry with my mother for not speaking to me about this important day. The woman in the front of the room tells the children, "This might be the most important day of your lives so far." She flashes a big white-toothed grin, meaning it's a happy day. I am also angry with my mother for not taking better care of me the way the other children apparently have been cared for. I make a promise to myself that I will not count on her anymore. That I cannot count on her. That I will take care of myself from now on. I promise myself that I will never feel ashamed of myself again, that I will learn how to look and behave by watching other people, who apparently know more than my mother. I promise myself that someday I won't feel inferior anymore. I will be the best, better than all these other kids.

By the time the class ends and the children return to the closet to gather their belongings, I have already pulled my socks up, pulled off as many nubs from my sweater as I can, smoothed down my dress, and, using my fingers, pushed my hair behind my ears. When I walk out of the closet, I believe that I am the only one the wiser.

I become a fan of paper dolls and love playing with them. These perfect girls allow me to dote and nurture, to use my imagination. I pretend to be the good mother and hold conversations with them that I wish my mother was having with me. "You're a good girl, Barbara," I say with a smile. "You make me happy." Other times I pretend to have stepsisters and a stepmother like Cinderella with the Prince who comes to find me. But most importantly, I learn how to dress by dressing them.

First of all, I take great care in cutting out their clothes. I work slowly and cut precisely along the edges. None of the white background paper shows or is left behind. All their outfits have to match. The pink sundress goes with the straw hat banded in pink, and the pink and white lace anklets. I press really hard, using my fingernails against the table to tuck the tabs in back where they can't be seen. That way the clothes do not fall off and look real when the dolls are standing on their hard cardboard mount. I place a high value on paper doll taste in attire. When I get older and can buy my own clothes, everything must match and look really neat, just like the girls in kindergarten.

The next year, I discover another game I like to play. School with me as the teacher. The idea comes to me when I go with my mother to the bank. I am just the right height to see the deposit and withdrawal slips in their cubby holes waiting to be filled in with numbers. I take a bunch and bring them back home with me and then outside to play among the neighborhood kids. When the younger kids see me, they arrange themselves on the set of stairs leading up to our building called a stoop. Some sit at the top row, some in the middle, and the rest on the bottom step.

I stand in front of them, hand out the papers, then read them a story about Dick and Jane. They love hearing about Spot the dog and his misadventures. They laugh and ask for more when I tell them the trouble Spot gets into. I change the story to make them the characters in it. They can't read yet so they get even more excited when they hear their own names.

"Run, Kathy. Run, Joe. Run and play." Or, "Go, Joe. Go, Kathy. Go. Go. Go."

I am six going on seven when we move from the Bronx to Canarsie, a neighborhood in Brooklyn. We are the first tenants in the new apartment. The building is very tall with an elevator to reach the upper floors. Our apartment is on the ground floor, so we don't get to use the elevator. Aside from being brand new, we have our own inside bathroom and no longer have to walk through one room to get to another.

There are a lot of buildings that all look the same on our side of the street. The apartment we live in is mostly empty with twin mattresses for my sister and me and one in the second bedroom for my mother. There is no other furniture or belongings. And no curtains on the windows. I can see people passing by on the sidewalk. All our clothing remains in suitcases. The rooms seem huge, and our voices echo when we speak. It doesn't look like anyone lives here. It is a strange all-white place.

No one ever explains to me why my father is not with us. I don't understand what is happening, and my mother won't answer any questions. I bug her one too many times asking where he is when she leans over me and shouts just inches from my face. Her full lips look swollen so close up. They are bright red and look scary like blood. Her voice, so filled with anger, sounds like it is going to crack.

"It's because of you. He left because of you. He loves me. If it weren't for you, he would still be here," she says, her larger body hovering over my smaller one, forcing me to crouch down backward.

I don't know how, but I know she is wrong. The more she screams at me, the more I want to prove her wrong. But instead, when left alone, I try to figure out what I did to make them both angry at me.

With the start of second grade, Rhonda, my younger sister by four years, and I begin the routine of seeing my father away from the apartment every other Sunday. He is not permitted inside and waits for us outside on the sidewalk. He picks us up in his car and takes us visiting. Sometimes we go to see his mother, Grandma Walters. Sometimes we visit a friend of his who talks to us and asks us many questions. She is very pretty and friendly to us.

One Sunday night, when my father brings us home, my mother is waiting behind the front door with her coat on, motioning to us not to take ours off. She shushes us, holding her finger across her lips, meaning we need to be quiet. She is standing tiptoe, peeking through the keyhole, watching for something. In a few minutes, she tells us we are leaving. My body freezes. I can't feel myself breathe although my heart is drumming loudly in my ears. The sound is so loud to me that I think everyone can hear it. When the new car she is waiting for pulls up in front, my mother rushes us out the door and throws our suitcases in the trunk. There is a man, a woman, and a boy already in the car. My mother gets in the front with the man and the boy. My sister and I sit in the back with the woman. Because it is nighttime and dark, I can't see any of their faces very well.

Only the woman speaks. She tells us her name is Grandma Cookie.

It sounds like a fun name. But then she says in a stern way, "We have a long ride ahead of us. Don't ask questions. Just go to sleep."

His name is Larry and so is the boy's. I have never met two people with the same name in the same family before. When we arrive in Florida, we all live in a house together. A house. Not an apartment. Larry Jr. is our new brother. Rhonda and I share a bedroom. Grandma Cookie and Larry Jr. share a room together. And my mother and Larry Sr. share a room together.

Grandma Cookie prepares our food. She makes lunches for Larry Jr. and me to bring to school. There is a refrigerator shaped like a toy chest in the back of the classroom where the kids flip open the top and put their lunches in when they arrive. That's because it is a lot hotter in Florida than it is in New York. It feels strange to wear shorts to school.

Other children live on our block. I only meet some boys. They wear shorts without shirts. They dare me to take my shirt off. I do but don't feel comfortable and lay down on the grass in front of the house to hide my body. I see my sister in the rounded window facing the street. She has no clothes on and is crying. I run into the house to see what has happened. Grandma Cookie is shouting.

Between sobs, Rhonda says, "I just wanted to see . . . if the picture in the bowl . . . went all the way through." My mother is screaming now. "Stupid girl turned the bowl upside down with the cereal and milk still in it. Made a mess for Grandma to clean up. And got her clothes soaking wet to boot. That's why Larry had to take them off."

I thought back to how embarrassed I was just taking my shirt off in front of the boys. Even though she's only three, Rhonda is made to stand naked in the window for all to see.

I wanted to say, "But everyone can see her." Instead, I mumble under my breath, pulling my head and shoulders down to hide from their reaction to my opinion.

"She deserves to be punished for what she did," Larry Sr. says. With that, he and my mother return to their room and close the door.

The next time their door opens, they are both in bed mostly covered by a sheet. They are talking to us, but something is strange. Their feet are showing, facing us from under the edge of the sheet. Their feet are in the wrong place. One of my mother's is on the inside next to a bigger man's foot. And the other two feet are also different, like their legs are crossed. This is a lot of firsts. The first time I see my mother in bed. The first time my mother talks to me for so long. The first time I see her happy in an even longer time. And the first time I realize something, I'm not sure what, very grown-up is happening between my mother and Larry.

Where's my father?! I shout in my own mind.

This becomes our pattern for several months. I am told to tell people at school that Larry Sr. is my father and Larry Jr. is my brother.

One day when I get home from school, I find my mother crying. Only my sister is there in the house. I learn that he left us. They left us. It's only been six months that we all had been together. I don't have enough time to think about what I will miss. Grandma Cookie's lunches? Walking to school with Larry Jr.? My mother says we are stranded with no money and no way to get home. What are we going to do? I sense my mother's fear and feel it for myself. The only time I have ever seen her cry before was when my father hit her. And this cry is different. She is wailing now.

It is never explained to me, but I learn later that my father sends us money to take a train home to New York. We no longer have our apartment in Canarsie, so we move in with Grandma Walters, my father's mom, who has a second bedroom. My mother, my sister, and I all sleep in one bed. And I start a different second grade class for the third time this year.

Chapter 3

After our return from Florida, the three of us live in the two-bedroom apartment on Hoe Avenue in the Bronx with Grandma Walters for the rest of my second grade and through the entire third.

I don't know where my mother disappears to during the day, but she always takes my sister, who is too young for school, with her. This leaves Grandma and me with time to spend together whenever I am not in school.

Grandma loves to teach me things they don't teach in school. Her specialty are lessons in "how to be a lady." Her living room serves a dual purpose, as a place for formal guests to congregate and as her office. In the corner of the room, off to the side of the chocolate-brown velvet upholstered sofa and dark blue glass-covered coffee table, sits a mahogany drop-front secretary desk. A workspace of her very own with golden handles. The lid of the desk folds down and forms a writing surface as well as reveals several small compartments for storing supplies, like paper, envelopes, cards, and writing utensils.

Sitting there side by side, we compose thank-you letters using delicate powder-blue parchment paper that makes a crinkling sound when we handle it. If you hold the paper up to the light, you can see right through it. Grandma whispers as though it is a secret between us, "The thinner the paper, the finer the writer." We practice our penmanship in script and fill our fountain pens from a jar of ink, soaking up the liquid as though our pens are thirsty. They drink through their straw when we lift the lever to refill them. The pens are shiny black with gold trim and feel heavy in my hand, like important tools. But their smooth surface also feels scary. *What happens if it slips out of my hand? What happens if I make mistakes?* This ink does not come with an eraser on one end, and I have only written in pencil before.

"Barbara, dear," murmurs Grandma as she leans her head closer to mine, peering over the top of her half-glasses, "all proper ladies express their gratitude and show their concern for others. There's no better way to say thank you or I hope you are feeling better than with a personal note." Then she waits until I show that I understand her instruction before continuing. "A person your age can write to a pen pal too."

Every day when I come home from school, I find Grandma sitting at the desk, writing in a little brown leather book called a Deskaide. "This is my diary, dear. It is private. That means it is only for me to see." She pauses to make sure I follow her meaning. When sensing my disappointment that she is not going to share anything more, she adds, "Maybe one day you will have one too. Then you can keep a record of all the important things that happen each day to look back on in the future."

After lessons, I know to expect formal tea each day at four without the tea but with Postum and tea biscuits. She prefers this caffeine-free roasted grain beverage that became popular after WWII when coffee was rationed. For lunch on weekends, she prepares miniature tea sandwiches, with the crusts removed, so that all that is left is soft little shapes filled with surprises. Her favorite is sardines. I never hurt her feelings by mentioning that their protruding little tails squelch my appetite. And the oily fish smell from the can seems to burn my nostrils. My tiny nibbles make Grandma proud, translating that I, too, know how to eat like a lady.

Then again, there is the "*hunt.*" I don't mean the sport, but Grandma's Yiddish word for her dog. Being so refined, Grandma often uses code names or spelled words, thinking I could be fooled. "Not in front of the *kinder,*" is one of her favorites. Or whispering "s-e-x" to another adult because she thinks I won't understand, ignoring that I am always a finalist in my elementary school-wide spelling bee. Grandma also never goes anywhere without a clean, pressed embroidered handkerchief. It is this love of cleanliness, order, and propriety that allows her to control a life that has been anything but controllable for a divorced woman of her generation, who all alone raised a rebellious son.

It is 1954 when we move to 615 Rosedale Avenue in the Bronx, a different move than the ones we made before. For one thing, my father rejoins us, the first time since our return from Florida. The four of us live together, my mother, my father, my sister Rhonda, and me. We have four rooms again—two bedrooms, a kitchen, and a living room. And we live on the fourth floor. I have just finished third grade and fourth will be starting in two months. I hope that four will be my lucky number. It is also the year that the words "under God" are added to the Pledge of Allegiance that we say in school every morning and also the year the Supreme Court rules that segregation in schools is unconstitutional. Only the change in the pledge affects me at this point. The rest will come later.

Our apartment is bright almost all day from sun streaming through the casement windows covered by sheer nylon curtains. They are called casement windows because they don't open all the way and only hinge outward for child safety purposes. The curtains sometimes get pulled into the openings depending on which way the wind blows and cast dancing shadows on the white walls. The living room and my parents' bedroom are decorated in light blond Formica furniture. My father's brother works for a company that makes the dressers and tables. Even my parents' bedframe. Everything is low to the ground with pointed corners, tapered legs, and shiny surfaces. My mother calls the Formica furniture "Danish Modern." To protect the sheen of the surface, my mother has each piece covered with thick green-edged glass.

I am fortunate enough to share a bedroom with a double exposure, one window facing front and another facing the side. From the vantage point of my bedroom, I can watch the entrance of our building and all the people who come and go, as well as those who live in the single-family homes across the street. The large lawn out front that reaches to the street is surrounded by a low white chain fence made of iron, with a circular sidewalk that is used as a bike path by the children in the neighborhood. Those that have bikes. I study the action outside from behind the light curtains in the safety of my room. Sometimes I pretend to be a spy, draping my body in the curtain like a cloak. Other times I simply observe wide-eyed, imagining how other people live.

Only three things in the apartment are not made of Formica laminate: my father's two large gun racks, the TV, and the twin beds in my sister's and my room. The beds are made of deep reddish-brown maple wood with spindles on the head and foot boards, high and dark compared to the rest of the apartment.

In this space, our eighth home in my nine years, hang the two open gun racks. Each are made of polished wood, with equally shiny guns and rifles straddling across their outstretched arms, as though they are being offered up to be taken and used. Copies of my father's paper targets, human outlines shot direct center through their heads, are taped alongside my 100 percent test papers on the refrigerator in the kitchen. He comes home bragging about how good he was. How he was the best shot. "Precise and accurately deadly," he says with pride filling his chest and taking up even more space in the room.

It is rare that all four of us are in the apartment at the same time because my mother now has an important job. Every day she styles her hair in a French knot updo, gets dressed up in her pressed pencil skirts with pleated slits in the back and matching two-piece sweater sets, and steps into her high heel shoes to go to the United Nations. She is a hostess in the "Delegate's Dining Room." I understand enough at age nine to conclude that the terms "United Nations" and "delegate" means that she has a very big job.

She never talks about her work. She does, however, ask me to massage her feet, hot and aching from standing on the job all day. It is unusual for her to engage with me, so I relish the chance to be close to her.

"Oh," she murmurs. "That feels so good. Do more of that." Or pleads, "Don't stop. Don't st-o-p-p-p." Occasionally, she compliments me as she lies back on the couch, resting her head on a pillow. I like pleasing her and can keep massaging for as long as she wants. Sometimes she is so relaxed that she even falls asleep.

Most other times at home my mother can be found reading, lost in a novel from the high stack on the low Danish Modern night table. Once, she brings home a stack of books from the library for me too. This makes me feel important, grown up, and happy.

Like my mother, I, too, can get lost in books, escaping to another life where girls can overcome their challenges and all problems work out in the end. When I am deep in a novel, my mother often calls, asking me to do something, needing help, and I never hear her. She could be standing right next to me. I can see her lips moving but her voice makes no sound that I can connect to. So wrapped up in the story I am reading, I am no longer present in the apartment. I find life in my books as satisfying as if I am in the middle of the story experiencing it for myself.

My father works, too, for the brother who makes the Formica furniture. On Sundays when my mother is at work, he makes us a hot breakfast. He fills omelets with any leftovers he can find or just seasonings and breadcrumbs. Then, too, there are the waffles, pressed round and brown from the waffle iron, the size of dinner plates. There is no syrup or butter in the house, so he covers them in peanut butter while they are warm, making them gooey and sweet. I love to fill each small square. Then cut them and eat them one by one, making the moment last.

FACING THE JAGUAR

In the evening, he pans a steak from my grandfather's butcher shop and tells us about his work. He is a big man compared with me but becomes even bigger whenever he tells a story. His body seems to inflate as he sits up taller and leans forward toward his audience. His eyes, like searchlights, watch our every reaction to his words of choice.

"I make machines," he starts, "that take the place of many men. That are smarter than men." Like the running of one of his machines, he's on a roll. "They are improvements in processes and efficiencies. The company would not be as successful as they are without me," he says, letting us know how necessary he is but also underappreciated. "They'd be lost without me."

Then, too, there is usually a dinnertime math quiz for me.

"Barbara, if one train is traveling north at 50 miles an hour and another train is on the same track barreling south at 60 miles an hour, given that they are currently 165 miles apart, how soon before they collide?" I am good at math. But as a visual learner, there is no way I can solve this problem in my head without paper and pencil. Plus, I am so afraid of having a wrong answer. I want to please him with the correct answer, knowing what could happen if he becomes angry.

"Come on. You can do it. You're going to be an electronic engineer someday," he adds, I guess thinking that this will encourage me. How can I tell him I don't want to be an engineer? How can I swallow my food with the huge knot in my throat? I don't want to disappoint him or make him mad. It becomes easier not to eat.

It is during these dinner talks that he shares his vision for my future. I realize the dream he had for himself that remains unrealized as a high school dropout. Hence electronic engineer. His topics cover other areas, too, ones he thinks I should know about now that I am getting older. So he also teaches me the "facts of life." He explains that when a man and a woman share food together, such as an ice cream cone, the man passes a seed to the woman and a baby is born. So much for being able to enjoy eating ever again with a person of the opposite sex. I do not know why he brings up this subject. It seems alien and weird.

My mother is absent during these family dinners. The only tension comes from my father holding me captive at the table.

"Promise me, Barbara," he says, craning his face toward me, so close I can smell the food on his breath. "When you get married, never let your husband eat alone. When a man works hard for his family, he deserves company. Not just a meal. And even if you've already eaten, you can still sit with him and ask about his day. Promise me," he demands, raising his already booming voice an octave louder.

Of course, the peaceful times do not last. When they are together in the apartment, my parents start to fight once again. The fighting grows proportionately worse as the gun collection grows larger. And so does the fear that he will use them if he gets angry enough. Beatings at the door become routine. Laying the groundwork for his outbursts, my mother stands each night at the ready listening for his key in the lock. Even before he crosses the threshold, she files her charges against us for our daily infractions: an unmade bed, getting a poor grade in school, not listening to her when she called us, some spilled milk.

"They don't listen. Reform school for them. They deserve to be punished." My mother's voice can be heard throughout the fourth-floor landing. The front door has not even been closed. In a matter of seconds my father's belt slips through his back pants loops to the front. Then, for effect, he folds it in half, snapping it across his other hand in the air. Our signal of what is going to happen next. All the while she screams as though she is trying to protect us. "Not in the face, Jay. They're girls. Not in the face, Jay."

I soon notice that when he hits us, he does not beat her. When it is her turn, my sister and I cower in the farthest corner, hoping to be forgotten, but watch him drive my mother to the ground with his fists. Blood, spit, and tears flow from her face. What can we do except close our eyes and shrink into the floorboards? I've known my mother does not take care of us like other mothers since that first day in kindergarten. Watching her complain about us to spare herself fills me with hatred for her.

Sometimes, my mother stands behind the sheer living room curtains watching for him to come up the walkway. We, too, watch him come up the front walk and run into our room, praying the thin wooden door will shield us from a pounding. Once again, she complains about "your lousy children" and screams, "Not in the face," when he begins to hit us. Sometimes, she retrieves his leather belt from the other room if he is not wearing it to punish us even more. We now have to pull our pants down for further emphasis and humiliation. Sometimes he misses my bottom and strikes leather or buckle to the back of my legs. Sometimes even between my legs.

Chapter 4

On most evenings, after he is sufficiently infuriated, my mother goes out, leaving us with him and the flames she has fanned.

I remember one occasion he does not let her leave, blocking her exit to the door. She runs toward the bathroom, which faces our bedroom. He chases her down the hallway, until there is nowhere else to run. Then he hits her until she falls to the floor, as she screams and spits at him, "I hate you," in between gasps for breath. "You'll pay for this," she hisses.

They have both moved so quickly in our direction that we do not have time to close the door. There is my father hitting my mother harder and harder the more she cries. My sister and I cry too. We beg him to stop. But when he turns toward us with rage, his face the color of fire and his eyes ablaze, we cower back in fear.

"Children should be seen and not heard!" He spews this out, his favorite motto, in what sounds like a loud roar. It never hits home the way it does that night. We have to watch but we cannot speak, as though it is a lesson for us in not making him angry.

It is never explained to us but shortly after this incident, my father no longer lives with us. I am given a door key and instructions. "You'll get a twenty-five-cent allowance for cleaning the apartment and walking your sister to school," is all my mother says by way of explanation. Over the next five years, my parents part frequently and reunite just as often. School becomes my sanctuary and I excel in fourth grade.

I guess I am just too busy reading to notice too much else. I am lost in a safe, cushioned, make-believe world. It is during this time that I discover the bookmobile, an old, converted school bus with rows and rows of books with different color bindings and titles facing out for me to consider. Like a child with their nose pressed to the window of a candy shop, I stare at the stacks of books barely moving or breathing. There are so many to choose from. Even ones higher than my eyesight. In my lifetime, I cannot get to all of them. Having trouble choosing, the librarian starts me on the Bobbsey Twins series.

"There are forty-six books in the series. That should keep you busy for a while," she says. "Two of the twins are younger than you. But two are older," she adds, looking down over her small square-rimmed glasses. I soon begin to feel like Nan and Bert, who are twelve, and Flossie and Freddie, who are six, are my friends, and later their parents are mine too. I find escape in their adventures.

At the same time the beatings end as my father no longer lives with us, my mother's disappearances begin in earnest. It starts as a day or two, gradually becoming a week, then a month. Not leaving us totally unprotected, she arranges for free school lunch and pays the next-door neighbor, Inez Cruz, to look in on us once in a while.

Mrs. Cruz is a kind, nurturing West Indian woman, with soft folds of flesh and wide angel wings that can encircle Rhonda, me, and her ten-year-old son Jimmy at the same time.

Because she apologizes so often, I believe she means well, but she is almost entirely preoccupied with Jimmy and the trouble he manages to get himself into. She is constantly being called out by the nuns at the Catholic school he goes to or worse, to the police station. When she isn't in those two places, she is in church praying for his soul. She even brings us with her on Sundays, two little Jewish girls who have never even been inside a synagogue. I learn to sing some hymns and put a coin in the collection basket while my sister, five years old, takes one out. (Years later, I would also learn how evil Jimmy Cruz really was when my sister recounted the acts he forced her to perform on him.)

Lucky for once, I start the first day of school with the rest of my class. My sister and I walk to PS 107, me in fourth grade, Rhonda in kindergarten. We have no breakfast supplies in the house but hold passes for our free lunch. It does not take me long to notice two things right away. Rhonda and I are the only white children in the free lunch line. And all the girls I know who also live in the low-income housing projects with us walk home at lunch time. I imagine to delicious lunches prepared by their stay-at-home mothers. I try waiting in line for lunch the first day, but I react physically to the cafeteria food. The cloying smell of boiling tomato soup and the hard, thick slabs of cheese and butter on the soft white bread force me, gagging and nauseous, to rush from the room.

Addressing lunchroom food concerns comes easily for me. I have the door key to our apartment. Thereafter, when my classmates leave school for their noon walk home, I join them, undetected by my parents or the harried free lunch coordinator. I return with my peers back to school as well, adding tales of my own mother and the wonderful lunches I share with her. No one knows I am missing from school except for my sister. And she is too young to know what to do about it. Besides, she is starring in her own drama by now.

Before long my favorite time of day becomes lunch hour. I walk home with the other girls then spend nearly the entire time in the quiet apartment, reading and dreaming, leaving just enough time to retrace my steps the three blocks back to school. Occasionally I lose track of the time. Then I run back so as not to be late. I want so badly to be good, and smart, and pretty. Everything I think the other girls are and would make my parents happy.

When I am left alone, when my parents are not at home, these are the most peaceful times. After I have read my library books two or three times, I hunt around for other things to read, even scanning ingredient labels on the scant items in the pantry. The short descriptions do not satisfy for very long. That's when I begin checking out the partial set of encyclopedias that my mother buys from the supermarket. Each month a new volume is for sale. But because we have moved so often, we never collect the whole set. We do get through the letter N, which feels like my own personal bookmobile and gives me a lot to read.

Some of the pages have multicolored photos. I love picturing myself in the exotic scenes, imagining what it would be like to visit or live in different places in the world, or different times in history. Over the next three years, I read nearly every volume, skipping over scientific topics, savoring ones that teach me something new about how other people live.

I learn what language words derived from and what years famous people in history lived. I learn about volcanoes and people from other cultures. Like an explorer, I read about international cities and how US holidays began. I love the world map section, wondering how many of these countries I will travel to someday.

Starting with the first volume, I read two pages about the first letter and first vowel in the English alphabet, A. I think it is just a one-letter word used frequently to denote one of something. I learn that it was a symbol long before our language was formed, originally found as a hieroglyphic in an ancient cave.

It lightens the heaviness of my home life to discover these facts. I have a connection to the outside world while I sit huddled on my bedroom floor reading, using the footboard of my bed for support.

About the same time, my fourth-grade teacher leaves the school and a younger woman takes over our class. Miss Colter is blond and pretty and very bouncy. She moves around the room, looking at us individually when she talks. Many of the kids pretend not to know the answers to her questions. Or that our previous teacher has not yet taught us that subject. They laugh and play dumb, thinking it will waste time and save them doing work. I see this opening as an opportunity to gain the favor of a grown-up. My hand frequently shoots up before anyone else's.

Then one day before sending us to lunch, Miss Colter gives us a poetry writing assignment. A collective group groan rises up from the boys in response. I do not know much about poetry, but in an attempt to impress Miss Colter, I run home to the partial set of encyclopedias. I remember reading a poem about Halloween. I copy it down and bring it back to school for her approval.

"This is great, Barbara. I am going to enter it into the school-wide contest." Her arm is waving as though she is holding a baton, not just my paper, in her hand. I feel happy that she likes what I brought in and scared that something is in motion that I cannot take back.

When Mr. Stein, the principal of the school, stops by our classroom and asks for me, I freeze inside. My stomach clenches and my breath stops momentarily.

"Come with me, young lady," is all he says, holding the door open, then leading the way to his office.

Mr. Stein pulls out a chair for me across from his desk before sitting in his own seat. "You are a very talented poet, Barbara," he says with a smile. "I don't know how to write a poem like this. I was hoping," he pauses and smiles again, "that you could teach me how to do it."

Why did I let Miss Colter think that I wrote the Halloween poem? I fret to myself. I took it from a supermarket encyclopedia thinking no one would recognize the author. Now I have to do something to get out of this fix.

"Here's a pencil and paper," Mr. Stein interrupts my thoughts. "I'll just watch you do your magic." With that, he gets up from his seat and comes around the desk to look over my shoulder.

Luckily for me, I have read that poem several times before copying it. I quickly compose a poem about Thanksgiving. Not as good as the original but with the same cadence and verses, the same rhythm and rhyme. Mr. Stein is not the only one who is surprised. I receive the poetry writing contest award and the respect of several of the fifth-grade teachers who offer me jobs assisting them in the next grade.

"Don't make waves," is one of my father's famous warnings. Yet he rolls in and out of our lives with the regularity of the tide. When he is home, the fighting escalates but so do the lessons. He talks to me about electricity while rubbing a balloon on my hair and watching it stick to the wall. For the school science fair, we build a volcano using the reaction of baking soda and vinegar to simulate lava flow. He draws diagrams of how the machines he builds use pulleys and levers to reproduce the effort of ten men.

Most of his talks end with the same warning: "You can't trust people, Barbara." His face shaking side to side, he says, "They screw you in business and steal your ideas." Watching his anger grow confuses me. He is the most powerful man I can imagine. The talks last for hours. Through it all, he lights one of his unfiltered Camel cigarettes. Then, before he has almost finished one, he turns it around and uses it to light up another one, filling the ashtray with small stubs stained yellow at the end like his fingertips. When I can't follow his technical train of thought any longer, I watch the smoke billow from his mouth and nose at the same time, imagining figures and objects forming in the vague shapes.

Between all the encyclopedias and my father's lessons, I feel myself getting smarter. I love going to school so much that some mornings I skip there along the sidewalk, humming to myself, forcing my sister to hurry and catch up.

It's not surprising that school becomes my safe place and I excel under some very inspiring teachers. Miss Colter and Mrs. Wiggs seem to think I am special and assign monitor roles to me. I become the chief messenger and paper distributor because I always finish my tests the quickest and can be sent to other classrooms or the principal's office on their behalf. Having earned the highest grades, my paper is the first one handed out, granting me the privilege of distributing the remainder, seeing the other grades before the actual takers do.

Arithmetic, reading, and poetry all come easily to me. Spelling becomes my specialty. Every week, Mrs. Wiggs divides the class into two groups, lining us up on opposite sides of the room. Alternating between teams, she gives the first person in line a word to spell. If we get it right, we go to the back of our line and remain standing for our next turn. If we spell it wrong, we sit down. I am invariably the last one standing. It is an easy victory. All I have to do is memorize our weekly spelling list and the extra credit words. There are no surprises. Due to my spelling prowess, I even earn the right to represent my class during the annual school assembly spelling bee competition.

It is no longer enough for me to wait for the bookmobile every other week. Leaving Rhonda with Mrs. Cruz and Jimmy, I take the bus to the local public library and visit my Grandma Nagler, my mother's mother, who lives nearby.

She is quite different from my other grandmother, though both are very loving and think the world of me.

"One day, mamaleh," she says in combined Yiddish and English, "you're going to be a lawyer and marry Eddie Fisher." Those are the two highest compliments she could give anyone. To someone who has never learned to read or write during their lifetime, a grandchild who can do both those things is extraordinary, especially at the age of nine.

She loves Eddie Fisher because he is Jewish. To me, "Oh! My Papa" can't touch Bill Haley and His Comets' "Rock Around the Clock," and I think Eddie is too skinny.

"You want I should make you some French coffee, Shayna?" Grandma asks. She thinks I am sweet.

What a special treat it is to be served Grandma's French coffee, a touch of coffee with loads of scalded milk, while discussing the meaning of life, as she understands it from the rabbi of her shul (synagogue), and sharing very grown-up activities.

Having just come from the library, time with Grandma is spent with me reading stories, writing my own and with Grandma illustrating them using her basic stick figures. Like Aesop's fables, she then acts out the moral of good versus selfish behavior. Even more fun are the times we dance in stocking feet, gliding and twirling across parquet wood floors to the console radio in the corner of her living room, taking turns with a triangular dust mop as our partner.

Grandma has a dressing table in her bedroom with a large oval mirror and a bench wide enough for both of us to sit down on. On her silver tray sits a pearl-handled hairbrush and handheld mirror as well as perfume, nail polish, and lipstick. This feels like movie-star luxury to me.

When we aren't writing stories or dancing, we fix each other's hair, squeezed together, whispering like two girlfriends. First, we brush each other's hair one hundred strokes. Grandma teaches me how to make finger curls by wetting a strand of hair and rolling it around my fingers. I feel so grown up and enjoy doing her hair and nails even more than having my own done.

I know she enjoys these times with me too. Especially when she confides about her own childhood.

"Maidelah," she calls me. "When I turned thirteen," she remembers with sadness in her voice, "I had to leave my family and go work on a farm. With thirteen children and no money, every one of us was given no choice and had our pay sent home." Looking down at her hands, she adds, "Our family could not exist on our own land."

Although she never says it, I later learn that the overabundance of laborers in Hungary at the time she grew up after WWI often resulted in maltreatment and abuse from overseers and landlords. Many of the peasant laborers had enough of the back-breaking work. They gambled everything on steerage to America because they had little to lose and everything to gain. The pull was further augmented by money and letters sent by relatives and countrymen already in America, providing testimony of the favorable working conditions and high pay in the United States.

Then almost immediately after arriving in America, my grandmother met my grandfather at an Austro-Hungarian dance. The start of my mother's family.

Chapter 5

One of the times that my father is not living with us, I contract the German measles. A week of lying in bed in the dark and trying not to scratch my itchy skin. On the first afternoon, my father comes to visit me. My mother takes her usual place behind my bedroom drapes, peering into the street. When he reaches the apartment door, she refuses to answer it, pretending that no one is home.

"I know you're in there," he says through the door. "I just want to see my little girl. I have a present for her. Promise I won't do anything wrong." How quickly I forget the beatings and feel love for my father. He brought me a present. I cannot remember the last time I got a present for any reason.

"I will not let him in," she whispers to me, bending forward so I can see her.

Through the door I hear him shout, "Tell Barbara I love her."

"I have a court order," she adds just to me as she leaves the room.

As soon as she is certain he has driven away, my mother opens the door and brings me the package he left behind. Inside are three hardcover books. Even though I am kept in a darkened room shielding my eyes from light and cannot read, I see they are brand new. The books I borrow from the bookmobile or the library are well-worn. I have never seen anything like these before. The covers are stiff and crackle when I flex them open. The written pages are silky smooth, untouched by any other child. I hold the books to my chest. I smell them, inhaling their delicious new scent. Even though they are rigid, causing some discomfort, I go to sleep with them under my pillow, savoring the moment when I will read them and travel through life with other families far away from home.

It does not take me long to start reading in spite of my bedroom being dark. As soon as my mother leaves the apartment and I am alone, I get out of bed to search for the flashlight my father uses to replace fuses in the front hall each time the electricity blows out. I know he keeps it somewhere nearby for those emergencies. Sure enough, it is right there on the shelf in the hall closet where I can reach it. Now prepared, I read under the covers, tented over my head, with a handheld spotlight leading the way.

Whether under the covers or out in the open, I start with *Anne of Green Gables*. I feel like the little orphan girl who's neglected and shipped from place to place. If she can ultimately find a home where she belongs, then maybe I can too. Next, I read *Nancy Drew: The Bungalow Mystery*. While Nancy is older than me, she is not only good at everything she undertakes, but also great at figuring things out. I want to be like her. The third book is the largest with 762 pages and that's why I save it for last. *The Complete Fairy Tales of the Brothers Grimm* keeps me occupied for a long, long time. While some of the stories are gruesome, I look for the moral in each one, thinking I might be able to avoid some pitfalls for the rest of my life.

It is 1956, and at eleven years old, I notice things when I stay still and observe. I can tell even before my father's anger escalates. He might start with banging his fist, slamming it down, or punching the table or a closed door. I can anticipate when my mother is preparing to leave even though her facial expression gives nothing away. She usually looks like the rigid stone masks the encyclopedia says were found at Mayan pyramid ruins. Her preening gives her away. Even when she bought the new record *Heartbreak Hotel* by Elvis, her favorite singer this year, her face remained rigid . . . although her lips parted making her look like she was going to say something but did not.

Another time when she does say something, her words seem foreign and make no sense to me.

"If you see a pink spot on your panties, call me," she says as she heads out the door of the apartment.

I am thoroughly confused. What could she possibly mean by that? I wonder but am not surprised. The opposite of my father, my mother is a woman of few words and even fewer explanations.

So, months later when I stand up in the bathroom and notice the toilet paper I used is red, I feel faint like all my blood has left my body from in between my legs. Frightened, I turn around and see all the water in the bowl is red too. Blood red. Panicking, thinking I cut myself on the toilet seat, I call my mother.

I scream as loud as I can through the closed door, "Ma!" then take a deep breath to repeat "*Ma!*" She does not respond. I wonder if I am bleeding to death. "Mommy, I need you. Help me, please," I plead. "*Help!*"

After several attempts, I need to reach the door to open it a little so she can hear me. Wadding a bunch of toilet paper in between my legs, I crack the door only to find my parents arguing from two rooms away. "Money . . . never home . . . cheating." My heart starts to race, scaring me even more.

This is a sign that she will be leaving soon. I must get her attention. "I'm leaving," I hear her say.

"Ma," I scream. "Ma!" at the top of my lungs. "Help. Please!"

This time, she steps into the bathroom.

"What is it?" she says with annoyance in her voice. I point to the toilet bowl.

"Here," she says as she reaches under the sink cabinet and hands me a rectangular white cotton pad without further explanation of what has happened to me.

"What do I do with this?" I ask quickly, seeing that she is getting agitated and wants to leave.

"Stay here," she says, leaving me alone. When she comes back, she has two safety pins. The first one she uses to attach a tab from the pad to the front of my undershirt. She attaches the second one to the back of my undershirt.

"What happened to me?" I ask softly, still frightened I did something to hurt myself.

"You've got the curse, silly girl. You must not wash down there. Promise me you will never get wet down there when you have it." She is finished and I remain standing there even more confused.

At school, there is one hygiene class in fifth grade where we watch a black and white movie that shows the birds and the bees pollenating flowers to explain reproduction. Mostly, there is a lot of snickering and giggling going on. Maybe the girls with older siblings can read between the lines. This school explanation feels useless, no better than what my mother had to offer me, which was nothing. Being the first of my friends to menstruate offers no other support. Eventually, my mother buys me a pair of rubber panties with metal clips in front and back to attach sanitary napkins. It is embarrassing to discover what they are called when she sends me to the drugstore to buy some for her. The pharmacist has to point out the shelf they are located on for me. So much for starting to feel smart.

"Come here, Barbara," my father calls from the master bedroom where he is sitting up on his bed. "I hear you've become a young lady," he comments as he pats the bed next to him, motioning for me to sit down on my mother's side. They are rarely home at the same time these days. She usually leaves shortly after he arrives home. She forbids me from being in their room except to clean it when she can sit and watch me.

At my father's invitation, I enter my parents' bedroom hesitantly. He motions again to the spot he wants me to sit. I try sitting to his left with my legs hanging off the bed, when he puts his arm around my shoulder, pulling me closer to him. "You mustn't turn out like your mother," he adds, not looking at me as though speaking to himself. "You must always do what your husband asks." He tightens the grip on my shoulder, and I feel my heart begin to race. I am confused when his muscular, calloused hand moves down my arm and grabs my left breast, squeezing so hard it hurts. "I'm going to teach you. Someday you'll thank me. I don't want you to be cold like your mother."

I swallow, not wanting to hear any more. Trying not to look at him, I turn my head. There on the wall next to us hangs one of the cabinets where his gun collection resides. The door is open and unlocked as though they are ready for use. That's when I notice a pistol and box of bullets sitting on the night table. I imagine him getting angry and using this weapon on me.

I say nothing, make no noise as I hold back tears that begin welling inside my throat and burning behind my eyes. All I can think of is my father's favorite admonition. In obedience, I silently repeat it to myself over and over again, *Children should be seen and not heard. Children should be seen and not heard.* He continues to talk but I no longer distinguish the words. My only saving thought is, please let this be over soon so I can go back to my books.

My mother seems to be gone most evenings now. There is good news in that. No more fighting. The apartment is quiet during the day and at night.

The first time I hear his footsteps coming into my room, I lay perfectly still and stiff, tightening every muscle, hoping he thinks I am asleep and will leave when I don't move. He sits on the edge of my bed and puts something soft and squishy in my hand. I refuse to take hold of it, not liking the way it feels flopping and slipping in my palm. That's when he presses his hand around mine and squeezes my fingers tight, moving my hand up and down, getting faster and stronger with each pump. I hear his breathing getting heavier and more rapid, like he is running up the stairs.

It seems like forever before a grunt escapes from him as some gloppy liquid oozes down my fingers. "I'll be right back," he says, making it sound as though I want him to return. He comes back with a wet cloth, cleans my hand, and says, "I'm doing this for you, because I love you. I'm doing you a favor." Then he leaves.

As my hand dries, I feel some caked-on film between my fingers. I want to get up and take a bath. I feel so dirty my skin seems to crawl. But I don't want him to see me awake. *What just happened?* I ask myself. *What did I do to make him punish me like this?* More importantly, I wonder, *How can I stop this from happening again?* I have to figure this out. I worry that I'm not smart enough to do that. *Is this my fault for being such a disappointment to him?* The only thing I am sure of is I don't like it. And all I can do is hold my crying inside so he doesn't hear me and come back.

The next time he visits me at night, he removes the blanket from my bed, takes off my pajama bottoms, then tries to separate my legs. I hold them so rigid and tight that he has to pull them apart and press his arms on top to hold them that way. I am terrified. My head feels like it will burst. In my terror behind closed eyes, I see a huge black cat lunging at me with flames shooting from its eyes and salivating fangs protruding from its mouth. Then I feel it licking me between my legs. I feel that feeling you get right before you throw up when your body's insides start reversing. I feel something else happening, too, that I do not want to experience. It feels like I am going to start shaking or worse, pee. I have to hold it back. I have to get away from what is happening.

Behind the blackness of my closed eyes, the cat I see turns into a jaguar. I am lost in the jungle running away from it. I cannot afford to feel anything. I will myself to feel nothing. I build a barrier around me. Nothing gets through. Do not feel. Even if it catches up, feel nothing.

"Someday you'll thank me for this, Barbara," he says before leaving. "I don't want you to be frigid like your mother." All I am grateful for is that I can finally relax my tensed muscles and exhale. Without realizing it, I have been holding my breath.

I use this recurring dream to help me get back to sleep: It is Saturday afternoon at four o'clock when I head to the public library. The building feels huge to me with stacks of books almost to the ceiling and rows of bookcases as abundant as trees in a forest. I find a copy of Willa Cather's *O Pioneers!*, then make my way to the farthest corner in the back of the fiction section where the authors' names start with the letter Z. Even though there are plenty of empty chairs, I squat down on the floor and begin to read. I imagine what it is like living during pioneer times. The never-ending chores to be done. The dangers of weather, terrain, and attack. The unknown. I feel strong like one of the female characters who wants to overcome adversity and succeed. In the background, I hear a soft announcement: "The library will be closing in ten minutes." I continue reading. In the distance I hear another announcement but can't make out the words. A few minutes later the overhead lights start to blink off and on. I feel safe and comforted in my corner of this world. I am not alone. Willa is speaking only to me.

When I finish the book, I wander through the rows and stacks of shelves building a long list of future books to read. I spend time looking through the small wooden drawers of the Dewey decimal system cards for ideas. I am euphoric.

My dream doesn't end until Monday morning when the lights come back on and the library opens once again to all its less fortunate patrons.

Chapter 6

I continue to fine-tune my observation skills, watching the way the people around me interact with each other. It never shows up as a good grade on my report card though. Anyway, it isn't long after the nighttime visits start that I notice significant changes in our household:

The beatings stop for everyone. There are no more for my mother, my sister, or me.

My parents do not separate again. Which means my father lives with us all the time now.

My younger sister is always in our shared room at night. I cannot be sure if she is awake or not when my father comes to my bed. The only exception is when we band together and ask my mother for a lock on our door. Of course, the answer is no.

It is Rhonda's idea to stack our metal roller skates against the door. This type of skate fits on top of our shoes and is adjustable with a bottom screw and a top key we wear around our necks. Through the adjustments, they are able to extend and fit different shoe lengths. With four skates and their metal wheels, we hope that a loud clatter will draw attention when the door is opened from the outside. This too does not work.

I do get a regular warning that my father will be arriving shortly when my mother says loud enough for me to hear, "Not tonight, Jay. Not tonight."

And the most important realization is that my father does not stay in my room whenever I am menstruating. Is that possibly an

44

explanation why I get my period every two weeks instead of once a month? It is at least the reason why I wear a lightly soiled sanitary napkin long beyond my flow.

I make the last change myself when I begin to keep a daily diary just like Grandma Walters. In it I write about my father's visits as best as my eleven-year-old vocabulary can put language to it. The diary is a typical pink leatherette with a tiny brass lock and an even tinier key that I keep hidden in the change purse I use to hold my allowance.

Dear Diary, He came into my room again last night and did things to me. I lay perfectly still hoping he would think I was asleep and leave. He didn't. He did say he'd kill me if I tell anybody. That this was our little secret. I am so afraid.

I don't know that there's a word for what's happening to me at home. That's why it comes as a shock to me when I discover it during one of my lunch-time encyclopedia reading breaks. The meaning of the word. What it is called. It falls in the encyclopedia after the Incas of South America and Incense that produces a fragrant smoke when burned.

Incest is sexual intercourse between persons who are usually prohibited from marrying because of their affinity or consanguinity.

The definition of what my father is doing does not mention the hurt, confusion, or fear. Nor does it describe what it does or what it feels like.

I quickly reach for the dictionary I keep near me when reading the encyclopedia and check out the two new words.

Affinity, a strong liking for or attraction to someone or something.

Consanguinity, the fact of being descended from the same ancestor.

Of course I know that my father is married. And although I'm supposed to love my parents, I don't want to marry him. Nowhere in this explanation does it say that what he is doing to me is wrong.

Or right, for that matter. What am I supposed to do with this new information?

My shame is so severe that I make a promise to myself: never let anyone see how terrible and damaged I am. And write a book of my own someday to help another girl from feeling so alone like I do. I dream of company and imagine there is another girl who longs for that too. I cannot see a solution for how to help myself yet but at the same time, I am sure that someday I will have all the answers. Like the heroines in the stories I gravitate to, even when events worsen their problems, they always triumph in the final chapter. Someday, I will overcome every challenge thrown my way. My final chapter will end happily too.

There is a boy in my class named Nathaniel Walters. While we have the same last name, we are not related. The kids in our class make fun of us, especially me for having an African American brother. I like Nathaniel. He is smart and a good person. Our teacher brushes off the jabs and tells us both to ignore them. But it still bothers me.

One evening over dinner, I ask my father what it means that Nathaniel and I have the same last name and what I should do.

In his big storytelling, dramatic voice, he extends his chest and lifts his upper body for emphasis. "We must have been plantation owners who had many slaves in our family background." He lights a cigarette and takes a long, dragging inhale then looks to see that he has my attention and gives me a knowing smile before adding his rationale. "When the slaves were freed, they only had first names. Blacks were not equal to whites. And the only last names they knew were those of their masters. So, they took our names as their own. That boy's family must have been our slaves." Satisfied with giving me a good description of the truth, my father relaxes back in his chair and goes back to his smoke rings.

I don't know how I know, but I know he is wrong. I think the story

FACING THE JAGUAR

47

he just told me is horrible. Everything about my father confuses me. Unlike the parental figures in the books I read, he does not fit into the good or the bad category. The worst part is that someplace deep down, I believe I need him. That I would stop existing if he were not in my life. He feeds me and teaches me to cook. He cleans the house and shows me the right way to do things. On weekends, he takes us for rides in the country. He is the only one around to watch over us these days and the only one who cares enough to talk to me even if the information is skewed. While I justify all this in my mind, I can't help also feeling, and worse, believing, that deep down I must be a very bad girl who deserves to be punished.

Is the stability I think I have worth the price I am paying? Without my father, we would go back to moving from place to place. Having to live with different people instead of having a place of our own where I can go at lunchtime and read. Teachers would not get to know me. There would be no food. No one to turn to or speak to. There would be no love. I think about escaping sometimes. But where would I go? He keeps us alone with him. We never see other people except at school. I doubt that other eleven-year-olds could help me escape. I imagine he might kill them too.

The next time my father comes into my room, I try sleeping on my stomach to discourage him. He forcibly flips me over. I squeeze my legs even tighter together. He pulls off the bottoms of my baby doll pajamas and uses what I guess to be his legs based on the weight to press mine apart. I am terrified. It feels like something rough and calloused is being drilled into me. Searing pain burns like fire from between my legs, up through my heart and throat. Until now, all his actions have been on the outside of my body. Now he's inside me. The pain that follows is unbearable. I can't stand it any longer and disappear into the densest, darkest core of the jungle.

I can see the jaguar chasing me and feel the heat of its breath. This time we run around in circles just like the tigers in a Golden Book I remember reading when I was younger. Instead of little black Sambo and the tigers circling each other around a tree, I'm the one who runs until exhaustion melts into butter and disappears. Like the father in the story, my father later collects the butter to enjoy on the pancakes he makes. Like Sambo, I trade my clothes for safety.

"If you tell anybody, I'll have to kill . . ." He probably thinks he's talking to me, but I have already left my body and the room.

This is the pattern of my life. School by day, jungle by night. It is during this time that I discover my mother is reading my diary. I am convinced she is reading the diary because there are things I do not tell her that she confronts me with. Things like exploring in her bedroom drawers when she is not home. Or trying out my aunt's lipstick one time when I go to her bathroom during a visit. Or agreeing to meet one of the Puerto Rican boys on a vacant lot behind the school where all the gangs hang out. Or smoking cigarettes. She tells me regularly now that I am a bad girl and deserve to be punished.

On the occasions that she confronts me about these and other childhood explorations, her threat is always the same: "Wait till your father gets home. Reform school. That's where you'll be going." Surprising, though, she never asks about my father's nighttime visits in spite of her inside knowledge. I feel even more betrayed by her.

Although there are a few girls I consider friends during this period, I grow tired of the frivolous things we discuss, like what another girl has worn that day or who gets tripped up for gossiping. I have already painted a glowing picture of my home life to them and am not interested in putting a new coat on it now. The only other person around is my seven-year-old sister. There is no one left for me to confide in. I wonder if maybe all girls go through the same thing with their fathers. Maybe that's why the encyclopedia mentions incest as a fact. Or the reverse. That it's all part of a secret society, an initiation, and no one is supposed to talk about it. I don't want to be the first to break the code. And I certainly don't want my father to have to silence me if I do.

It is springtime 1957 and we are standing in front of the butcher shop my mother's father owns, waiting for the elevated train to continue on its way before speaking. The sound overhead is deafening. People are scurrying in front of us on their way home or to errands, loaded with bags of groceries. I am reading the signs in Grandpa's window: CHICKENS 39 CENTS A POUND. SMOKED HAM 63 CENTS A POUND. The banner sign over the window reads: HIGHBRIDGE MEAT MARKET. MEATS OF THE BETTER KIND. I feel proud that my grandpa owns this store. At last a train leaves the station and the noise level abates.

"You know you're Jewish?" Grandpa Nagler asks as I show off my new Easter coat and bonnet. He has given my mother the money to use toward clothing for my sister and me. At twelve years old, I think it is right to tell him this is what we got and say thank you before we leave.

"I am?" His question surprises me. I've heard of different religions. But nobody has ever told me which one I am before. And while Grandma Nagler has spoken to me about her rabbi, we go to church with our sitter, Mrs. Cruz. We sing the hymns with her. I feel part of that group. That's where I figure I belong.

Grandpa turns to my mother and questions her next. "Lillian? Why don't these girls know they're Jewish? We didn't escape the horrors of Europe to hide who we are here in America."

My mother's answer is ready immediately. "I don't believe in religion anymore."

"That might be fine for you, but these girls need to know where they come from," Grandpa insists.

"I didn't like the restrictions of the kosher home you raised me in," my mother responds in explanation. Then adds, "I can barely afford to pay my bills let alone pay for additional religious education."

"Then I'll pay for it."

The nearest synagogue to our school and the housing projects where we live is an Orthodox shul. And since we will be released early from school on the days the Christian kids go to catechism, Rhonda and I need to able to walk there on our own. So Orthodoxy is the only decision to be made.

When we join, there are no other girl students in the school. The rabbi in charge is inconvenienced by our presence. He starts by rearranging the classroom. Not only do the moving chairs make a lot of noise, but his huffing and grunting accompanies the scraping of the wooden floor.

In order to keep Rhonda and me separate from the boys, two rows of empty chairs are placed in between us and them. We are the furthest distance away from our teacher that is possible in the room.

My sister is having a hard time being ignored. Rhonda is fidgeting and talking to me while the rabbi is trying to teach a lesson about Passover. He is explaining the purpose of the seder, when Rhonda's hand shoots up.

"What's a Seder?" she asks.

Rabbi answers her question with two of his own. "Haven't you girls ever been to a seder? What kind of Jewish girls are you?"

I am floored how Rhonda knows what to say, but she finds a way to irritate the rabbi even more with her answer. "We have never been to a seder. Don't even know what one is. And our father makes bacon and eggs for us every Sunday morning for breakfast."

"Out," screams the rabbi, his outstretched arm pointing to the door and his face swelling with anger and frustration.

We get thrown out of religious instruction the first week. When

Grandpa Nagler hears about this, he makes a large donation to the synagogue and a rabbinic student is hired to teach us privately.

One other girl from the neighborhood joins our small group. We enjoy the classes with the young man in the thick black beard and head of curls to match. We mostly read Bible stories and discuss the moral to each story. Sort of like my *Grimm's Fairy Tales*. Because the new girl and I are older, we are also required to attend Sabbath services each week as part of our education.

That Saturday morning is the first time I enter the sanctuary. The walls are all paneled in dark wood, including the ceiling. There are rows of benches with a platform in front. A few men are standing on the platform with the rabbi and humming prayers in Hebrew.

I never find out why, but on this Saturday when I go to services, the other girl is not there. As a matter of fact, only one other woman is in attendance as I am pointed to the curtain-covered balcony up a flight of stairs in the back of the hall.

There are rows of seats here behind the partition. And I take one off to the side as I look around. The other woman is reading from a book, so I pick one up for myself. It is written in Hebrew, strange letters that I can't translate. I listen to what the men are saying. It makes no sense to me with only one week of religious instruction and Bible stories since then to go on. Looking around I spot a stained-glass window with unusual shapes in primary colors. The light from outside filters in differently through each color. I move next to the window to see if I can look through the glass.

I don't know how long I am daydreaming, listening to the droning melody coming from downstairs in the men's section, following the filtered light across the rows of seats, when it happens.

Something crashes through the window. It takes me a second to recognize a brick at my feet. I twist my head up to search through the fractured window where I see two boys running away and laughing. My head is spinning. This is not a nice thing to do. This is an act of hate. *How and why would they hate me? Is it because I am Jewish?* I wonder. That can't be. I didn't even know I was really Jewish myself until last month.

When Grandpa hears about this incident, I am set free from religious instruction, indefinitely.

By the time I am thirteen, I begin smoking regularly and hanging out in deserted lots with some of the less studious kids after school. Here the conversation comes closer to what I need to learn about: sex. Not exactly my experience, more of the kissing, groping variety of sex. I even have my first French kiss with that Puerto Rican boy of my diary fame. While I feel nothing, I like his attention. Which ends when my mother slams the door on him after he comes to call for me the next day.

"He's not white!" she screams. "Good girls do not make friends with dark boys." And in the same irritated tone of voice adds, "They don't lie. And, they don't smoke."

"How would you like to have a baby brother or sister?" my father asks my sister and me. He has called us into the living room to talk, and we both shake our heads no. There isn't enough of anything to go around. Food, room, love, parenting. I am fourteen now and Rhonda is ten.

Seeing our displeasure, my father explains his reasoning. "I need a boy to carry on the family name. And I want to get your blessings."

What my sister and I want is moot anyway. We didn't realize our mother was already pregnant. She is around so infrequently that we did not notice any changes in her appearance. Exactly four months after our first conversation about another sibling, our brother Rob is born. I am annoyed at my father for treating me like a naïve child who doesn't know pregnancy lasts nine months. Apparently, he forgets that I can add. Or maybe he is covering up the fact that my mother is no longer frigid, his rationale for coming to me.

FACING THE JAGUAR 53

In spite of not wanting another sibling, or at least preferring another sister that we can dress up like a living doll, Rhonda and I find baby Rob to be a surprisingly welcome addition to our family. He is small, adorable, and easy to love. What's more, he learns to return our love and affection at an early age. His bright eyes open ours to the raw possibility inherent in children. Our brother is born smart, and as soon as he is able to, he repeats the words to songs and stories we teach him, letting us gloat like proud parents. The three of us behave like a real family. That is until my father gets home.

"Where's my little prince?" he asks as he walks through the door, a big smile on his normally tired face after a tough day at work. He tosses Rob into the air and catches him back to safety followed by a big hug. Even before he sits down to dinner, my father spends time playing with Rob, questioning each new accomplishment and discovery. He no longer asks about our day or schoolwork.

Needing an extra bedroom prompts another move. This time to a block with many six-story apartment buildings that's close to the junior high, which includes ninth grade in this school, and the elevated train as a new form of transportation.

The move to Davidson Avenue is a step up from the low-income housing projects we leave behind. Our apartment building has a courtyard in front with a cement statue and fountain at its center, no longer operational, but grand nevertheless. Half the windows of our apartment face the court and the other half face the street. I continue my habit of sitting by the windows watching life move past, once again learning the ways of the street. The majority of the people here seem to be white and mostly Jewish, unlike the population of the projects. The smells that emanate from the various apartments remind me of Grandma Nagler's cooking. Rendered chicken fat, gefilte fish, and chopped liver with fried onions fill my nostrils as I climb the five flights of stairs, too young and energetic to wait for the elevator that moves like a turtle.

Starting ninth grade in the middle of the year is tough. Most of the students have known each other from at least seventh grade, if not as far back as elementary school. I am uncomfortable being the new kid on the block, having to pass everyone's initial inspection, especially being as physically gawky and awkward as I think I am. That's when I meet Karen. Karen Sue Steinberg is the previous new kid in town and is grateful for a chance to pass the title. At five foot eight, with carrot red hair and large brown freckles, she is still hard to ignore. But our newness works to bring us together. It is not the cause for our ultimate bond, though.

One day as I pass Karen in the hallway between classes, she whispers that she has a terrible family secret she wants to share with me after school.

Chapter 7

After passing Karen in the hallway, the day drags on in slow motion. I shift my thoughts to my luck in befriending her. At last, someone is going to validate my home life, the secret society that I wonder if all girls are initiated into, that betrayal of our bodies from childhood to adulthood. I now have a friend who wants to share her family secret. And I want to think of what my father does as an initiation, although he never calls it that. I long to tell someone, but I don't know what will happen if I do. Is it really a secret society, as I suspect? Might Karen be the one I will finally ask, the one who will legitimize my home life and let me know that I'm not alone?

The next few classes that I usually find interesting now bore me. Wishing to hurry the day along keeps me even more aware of how little time has passed. Sitting at my desk, I notice for the first time how every classroom is decorated with a large round clock above the blackboard displaying an exaggerated second hand. I actually think I hear the click the seconds make as I mentally count them to maintain some control over my anxiety.

In the three years since my father began initiating me, I have told no one about it. Unless you count my diary. What would I say to Karen though? After the first few times, I went deep into the jungle, separating my body from the experience. I wouldn't know how to explain it. Who would believe the jaguar chasing me? And knowing my father's violent nature, who could do anything about it that would not make the situation worse? I calm myself down by realizing if Karen is going through the same thing, no words will be needed to tell her about it even though she has not said as much.

The only classroom without a clock that day is Mrs. Lindemann's dance class. Set up like a studio with wall-to-wall mirrors and dance barre, I consider myself fortunate to be accepted into it. All the other girls have years of extracurricular dance, classes like ballet, tap, and modern. I have none. There is even more good news in being part of this class: I don't have to wear the baggy green gym suit or change in a crowded locker room. Now I wear a black leotard and tights under my clothes on dance class day. And the class is during regular school hours. I saved up my allowance to buy a pair of ballet slippers but could not afford the wraparound skirt that is part of the required class outfit. Instead, I bought a Simplicity pattern ballet wrap skirt and cut and sewed it myself. The inexpensive fabric I bought does not lay or flow as well as the ones from the dance apparel store. But I feel beautiful in it. Like my body is as it's meant to be.

Daydreaming through math, the last class after dance, I think of the new present Grandpa Nagler sent me: a portable Victrola record player. It is housed in a small turquoise suitcase with white trim and handle. And I can carry it anywhere along with a smaller suitcase that holds my 45s. I am always careful to place the arm and needle gently down on the record so as not to scratch it. Now, in addition to reading when alone, I love to dance around the apartment to music. When I'm melancholic, I listen to Little Anthony and the Imperials' "Tears on My Pillow," or its flip side, "Two People in the World." When I'm happy, it's Danny and the Juniors' "At the Hop." My body feels free when no one is looking. I daydream about boys asking me out on dates and to dances. My imagination gets me through to the end of the school day.

Karen and I agree to meet in our secret hiding place below the section of Davidson Avenue we live on. Our block is separated from the nearest parallel street by a huge elevation, like living on top of a very large hill. Every few blocks, long concrete stairways connect Jerome Avenue to Davidson, allowing subway and bus riders to take a shortcut home rather than walk several blocks around out of their way. Some of these staircases have seventy-five steps up to our block. We like to hang out there, perched under the stairwell hidden from plain sight.

At the very end of Davidson Avenue, one additional stairway leads to the street adjoining the Cross Bronx Expressway. This one is used the least because there are no shopping, stores, or mass transportation stops on the service road, which was added many years after the original construction. Only hundreds of cars speeding toward the George Washington Bridge and New Jersey. Karen and I decide to meet in a recessed portion of this stairwell, our secret place, as soon as school is over. It is in this dark cavern where I wait what seems like another whole day for her.

Karen arrives panting. "Sor-sorry," she gasps, crouching down into the cement hideaway. "The bitch . . . kept me," she adds. "She always finds jobs . . . for me to do . . . after school. I think she makes lists . . . all day long . . . and just waits . . . for me." Karen heaves a big sigh and plunks down next to me.

"It's okay," I say. "You're here now. That's all that matters." I pause, searching for the right words to encourage Karen to talk, to speak first of secrets and burdens. "I'm really glad you said you wanted to meet to talk about a terrible family secret." I look into her beautiful face, sorry that she might be feeling the same pain. "I have wanted to tell you about my family too," I whisper, the heavy weight on my chest threatening to crush me if I don't get out what I need to say.

"I knew it. I knew we had the same secret. I could tell," Karen rambles as she digs into her jeans pocket and takes out a paper package of sewing needles and a book of matches. "Let's take an oath first. Let's become blood sisters." She strikes a match and holds it to the tip of one of the needles.

My heart is pounding. A pulse throbs in my right temple, like a tribal drum providing the background beat for this ancient ritual. My senses are so heightened, yet I barely feel the needle prick my fingertip. But when Karen holds our bloody pinpoints together, I imagine waves of her energy dancing throughout my body. We are one.

"Okay. Now let's talk." Karen has called this meeting and led the proceedings so far. It is obvious she intends to go first. "Mrs. Steinberg isn't my real mother," she begins. "My real mother ran away and left us with my father when I was six and my brother was four. She was a real beauty, my mother, and an artist. My father met her in Australia while he was in the service." Without stopping for a breath, she continues, "She wanted to come to America but never really fit in. She was much younger than him and just picked up and left one day. He tried to contact her, to bring her back. But she wouldn't even return his letters or calls. He never got over her. And he couldn't stay home and watch the two of us and support us at the same time. So he found someone to babysit. Eventually she complained so much about us disobeying her that she convinced him to marry her so we would have a legitimate reason to listen to her. He once told me that he knew she would never run away because she was old and ugly, not like my real mother."

I listen in fascination as Karen unravels her story, at the same time wondering what any of this has to do with me.

As though she has been reading my thoughts, Karen ties the two together. "I can see by the way your mother treats you that she's not your real mother either. And it's very obvious that your father loves you but is too obligated to her to control the bitch."

I love my new friend for wanting to let me in on her secret, for seeing in me something she connected to, but I'm also crushed that our family secrets are so different. *Maybe she is holding back*, I think. *Maybe if I confront the issue first, she will chime in too.* "Karen, Lillian is my real mother. Unfortunately," I add, letting go of the tightness in my chest. "My terrible family secret is a little bit different. My father," I hesitate, not wanting to hear my voice describe out loud what he is doing to me. "My father," I try again and plunge forward, "has sex with me."

"What?" She jumps in closer both physically and with her thoughts. "How is that possible? Does your mother know? What is she doing about it? What are you going to do about it? Why would he do that? Doesn't he know that's wrong?" Her questions fly past me before I can even frame one answer.

"He sneaks into my bedroom at night, after she refuses him, after she wants to be left alone or goes out with her friends. I haven't told her because I'm afraid of what might happen if I do. They'll send him away and I'd be left alone with her, and that would be unbearable." Karen's face mirrors my upset, what I guess mine looks like as she moves in closer to me. "You were right," I say in confirmation. "She treats me like a servant and only talks to me to give me orders or criticism. I am so alone when he is gone. I don't know if you'll be able to understand this, but it is worse without him." I wait for Karen to take in all I've said.

"I love my father and feel sorry for him that his life turned out this way, so I can understand," Karen says. "And I know your mother is a monster too. Did you," she looks down at her hands and hesitates before asking, "did you ever tell your father that you might tell someone what he's doing?"

How could I tell my friend that my father has threatened to kill me if I tell and still explain why I believe I am better off with him than without him? I am not sure I understand it myself. "He tells me that someday I will appreciate what he is doing for me. That I won't end up frigid like my mother. That if I tell anyone what he is doing, they will send him away and my baby brother will be fatherless." No matter what I choose, I lose, I realize in that moment.

"Wow! Here I wanted to talk to you about how terrible my life is and your life is much worse than mine."

This says aloud what I have already been thinking. Plus Karen's confession bursts my illusion of a secret society of girls being initiated by their fathers. I feel even more alone after telling her mine and not being able to share the same secret.

"I wish I could do something to help you, but I don't know what to do," she laments. Karen takes both my hands in hers and I hold back no longer. Tears overflow from my eyes down my face from as deep as my toes as sobs burst from my throat. Her long arms embrace and wrap around me so that I can feel her crying, too, her young heart full of compassion for me.

After a while, Karen breaks the silence. "I have an idea. Why don't we form a secret club? You have to be a teenager with parent problems to join. We can have nicknames and initiations and we can be the leaders." She looks at me with eyes that hold hope for the future and for the resolution of our problems, waiting for my approval. How can I say no? "I'll be Cherry Pie, like the song," she laughs, "and you'll be . . . let's see . . ."

"Butch," I say. "Everyone will think I'm tough. That way no one will mess with me." What I really mean is if I have a boy's name and act like a boy, nobody will want to have sex with me. Including my father.

Karen and I graduate that June and begin our three years at William Howard Taft High School off the Grand Concourse in the Bronx. Starting at a new school brings some changes, and some things stay the same. The best part is Mrs. Lindemann, our beloved dance teacher, moves up with us. No more gym suits—ever. Secondly, Karen and I expand our club for girls with parent problems. Stephanie has two deaf parents. She has extra responsibility in communicating for them and is embarrassed by the sounds they make when they do try to

FACING THE JAGUAR   61

communicate verbally. Ronnie is an adoptee, and her aging parents are overprotective. Catherine does not know where her parents are. She is being raised by an elderly grandfather and uncle. I am part of a community, a group of friends, and spending more and more time away from the apartment. Mine is never the meeting spot. We congregate where there are either no adults, gone during the day at work, or at Stephanie's where her parents treat us special. They supply us with homemade treats and then leave us alone, giving us lots of autonomy.

Thanks to Mrs. Lindemann, Karen and I get dancing parts in the school play, *The King and I*. I join an after-school group called Junior Achievement where I learn about the business world. My day life feels like a typical teen's as soon as I begin dating. My nights remain the same. I mostly ignore them. I bury them in the big black hole I sink into when the lights go down and I can no longer see or feel anything. I continue to have a menstrual cycle twice a month which gives me peace at least half the time.

I meet Donny standing at the bus stop on the Grand Concourse waiting for the bus to take me home from school one day. As usual, the bus is late in coming and I am shifting around, impatient to get started on my homework.

"Hi there," he says like he knows me, smiling and lighting up his blue eyes, forcing a curl to slip down on his forehead.

Two thoughts cross my mind: *Boy he's cute*. And, *Don't stare*.

"I hope you don't think I'm being too forward, but you have a few stitches coming loose off your pocketbook."

I'm grateful for an excuse to look away and see that he is right. My first-ever new leather bag, which I saved up for until I could afford to buy it at Alexander's Department Store on Fordham Road, is unraveling at one of the seams.

As way of explaining, he adds, "I couldn't help but notice

because my father manufactures leather purses for a living." Then he shrugs his shoulders innocently as though he really couldn't help himself. "If you have a few minutes, we can stop up at the house now and get it fixed. Or you can come back another day if that's more convenient."

Holy cow, I think. *What's going on here?* No one is ever this nice to me, especially a stranger.

"On second thought," he continues, "why don't we go out, say for Chinese food sometime, and get to know each other better." It's like he is reading my mind.

Who is this guy? Did I dream him up? Before I can formulate an answer, he jumps in again. "Am I going too fast? I didn't even get your name or give you mine. I'm Donny."

I recognize the school jacket he is wearing. It's from the all boys' high school De Witt Clinton and realize that's probably why he's so glad to make my acquaintance.

Donny is everything he seems to be. The clean cut, all-American, charming only child of two loving parents. Upon meeting them for the first time, they move four chairs together to form a tight circle to be able to sit facing us and talk. They ask many questions, interested in everything about me. Where did I grow up? What does my father do for a living? How many siblings do I have? What are my favorite subjects in school? What do I like to do after school? All the while, Donny's father hand-stitches the loose threads on my bag, complimenting my wise purchase as a quality item. I have never met a family like this and feel so accepted and happy.

On our first date, Donny and I go out for Chinese food like he suggested. And after, he takes me home by taxi. Another new experience.

We continue like this for a while, going out to eat or to a movie over the next two months. I enjoy being treated so well. Then one time Donny brings me home and asks if there is someplace private we can go. The only private places I know are the laundry rooms in the basement of every building on the block.

We find an empty one across the street from my building and walk down into the darkness. Being the polite boy he is, Donny asks if he can kiss me. I nod yes.

I don't think Donny knows how to kiss a girl because I feel nothing. Just pressure on my lips. When he doesn't get a reaction, Donny asks if he can touch my breast. Again I nod yes.

Again I feel nothing. I stand frozen on the spot, numb to his hand but hearing his breathing become more pronounced and faster. I need to go, to leave. I don't like the place my mind is receding to. But I can't move.

In the dark basement, there are chemical smells and clanging boiler sounds, and creatures scurrying across the cement floor. I am being chased again. Running for my life. Disappearing farther and farther into the thicket. Waiting until it is over and safe for me to return to the surface.

When he is done touching me, we leave the basement. In the daylight again, we say goodbye but never see each other again.

These cha-cha steps will form a dance routine that I perform for the next five years with a whole series of boys from the neighborhood. I want to be liked. To please them. I don't know what else to do.

1, 2	*Whatever they want.*
1, 2, 3	*I withdraw.*
1, 2	*I feel nothing.*
1, 2, 3	*I show no reaction.*
1, 2	*No one gets inside.*
1, 2, 3	*I wait for it to be over.*

Leslie, Bill, Steven, and Robert are boys on the block, and they're next. After I meet Lenny one summer, he introduces me to his friends

Phil, Fred, and Mel. They pass me around like a lone, last cigarette, taking their long drag, then stubbing me out.

Chapter 8

The movie, *Where the Boys Are*, gives me hope. I picture myself in college on spring break, dancing in clubs or on the beach with my friends. I am especially attracted to one of the male stars in the movie, George Hamilton. He is so dreamy looking with his dark hair and piercing eyes. I am surrounded by plenty of other fantasy heart-throbs as well. A perfect assortment for a girl who thinks about boys liking her every chance she gets. I daydream about going steady with Frankie Avalon whenever I listen to my 45s of "Venus" and "From Bobby Sox to Stockings," picturing myself having left home and being the person he sings his love to. Then, too, there is Fabian on *American Bandstand* and *The Ed Sullivan Show* driving all the girls wild. The way his eyes light up and sparkle when he smiles makes me feel like his gaze is directed only at me. It doesn't matter to me that he mostly speaks the words to the songs he sings.

More and more now, when I get the chance and I'm alone, I dance around the apartment rather than read. How can my literary heroes, Pip from *Great Expectations* and Holden from *The Catcher in the Rye*, compete with the feeling of freeing my body through music and movement? Though I do practice my social skills in the bathroom mirror, aka Holden Caufield–style. Whether holding a cigarette or talking with a handsome boy, I learn by playacting and imagining an audience at the same time.

All my schoolwork is now getting done on my new portable typewriter. And I try my hand at writing poetry. It's on Grandpa Nagler's gift of the Royal that I compose an ode to him the day he dies.

Down cried the skies,
the day he died.
They too were sad.
Not more than I.
Will the sun never shine,
or the sky be blue?
Know we'll meet again,
when my time is through.

My mind is so flush with the power at my fingertips on the keys that I believe I can be a writer one day.

This is an exciting year for me in high school. I get an invitation from my guidance counselor to act in a summer stock company, and I get to take an elective art class. Those two new choices, plus the representative from Junior Achievement who spoke to us at an assembly about getting hands-on business experience, make the future feel full of possibility. So many options.

Things are still troubling at home, though. My father is away most days since he left his job and started his own company. The good news is that his night visits only happen once or twice a month between his schedule and my menstrual cycle. When he pulls down my baby doll bottoms and sees a sanitary napkin, he quickly exits my bedroom. My mother, now in charge, pushes back on everything I want to do. She refuses to allow me to go to summer stock. "I know what happens at those places," she says, and she narrows her eyes when she says this, her tone suggesting that nothing good can come from the experience.

When I try to get my father to agree, he shrugs his shoulders. "I'm not getting involved between you and your mother," he says, dismissing the subject and my feelings.

With her new power, my mother tries to hold me back even from typical things that girls want to do. I begin to get invitations to sweet sixteen parties, luncheons in restaurants with groups of girls, or coed dances in American Legion halls. I ask my mother what plans I can make for my sixteenth birthday.

"You can have three friends over here," she quickly answers. "With cookies and Kool-Aid." The silence that follows is deafening as I feel my body tighten into a knot.

I start to say "but" when she shuts me down.

"You're lucky we don't send you to a reformatory with your cutting school and smoking."

Once again I am stunned. There is no way for her to know about my cutting school unless she's read my diary.

"Let me smell your hand," she demands, grabbing my right. "I can tell." She separates my fingers and holds them up to her nose and inhales deeply. This is a small victory because I always smoke with my left hand.

Then, too, she forbids me shaving my underarms or legs even though I have heavy, unwanted black hair growing in both places. When the kids at school tease me, I am doubly embarrassed. My mother's rationale is that only hussies shave to attract the wrong kind of attention. I stop wearing sleeveless blouses and wear tights even in summer.

She leaves no room for discussion, and it leaves me split in two. I get the message that I am undeserving of anything good, anything that other people have. And I want to prove her wrong. I'll show her how good I am even if she doesn't think so. Later I think about how she calls me a hussy but denies reading my diary, which describes her husband's visits to my bed.

Sometimes I am so frustrated by what I judge as my mother's senseless need to control me that I think about how to fight back. The one thing she can never take from me and I can still control is how little food I eat and can manage on. I feel high experiencing my hunger, knowing that neither parent can get there.

Just when I think it can't get any worse, I lose bathroom privacy after my sister accidentally knocks over a bottle of milk. My mother is ready at the door to fire up my father when he gets home from work. Rhonda runs into our one bathroom and locks the door to hide from his rage. When he can't get her to open it on his command, he begins to beat the door down with his fists. First all the white paint chips off the door at the place of impact. Next come pink shards of shiny enamel. Then the green slivers fly off. For a moment, I wonder who lived here before us and painted the door all those colors. But I'm brought back to my sister's predicament when I notice the light filtering through the crack, and he pummels it even harder until he has broken more of the wood and plaster away. We have no privacy in our one and only bathroom after that. The door and my sister are both beaten down over spilled milk on the kitchen table. When I feel confused or defeated by my parents' behavior, I feel like that door. Beaten through the center with a big crack in my midsection and not enough of anything to ever cover or fill it. I feel hollow and exposed. Like people can see right through me. And as proof that there is nowhere to hide, the door will remain unrepaired for a long time.

No one ever talks about my father's rages, or about my mother's infidelity or her passive aggressive behavior, or about the night visits. So, in addition to the direct messages—*I won't be frigid; Rob will be fatherless; I will be killed*—there is an unspoken family message: *If we don't talk about it, it doesn't exist.*

Between sharing a bedroom with Rhonda and the crack in the bathroom, the only privacy I have is when I am either alone in the apartment or out in a crowd of people. I begin to enjoy my own company more and more and spend less time with other girls.

I try to find privacy elsewhere, spending most afternoons at the library. The only person I trust is Karen. One time when we are alone at her house, she teaches me how to get rid of my unwanted hair

FACING THE JAGUAR 69

using a depilatory cream called Nair. It has an obnoxious odor and burns when I wipe it off, but it works. At least I don't have to lie when my mother asks if I shaved.

My parents are the biggest embarrassment in my life. They are hypocrites. At dinner one night, they tell my sister and me that we cannot go to college. They reason that since neither of them graduated from high school, a high school diploma is suddenly a sufficient accomplishment for girls. True, I had never wanted to become an electrical engineer, something they'd supported prior to now.

In addition, they tell us, all their savings have to go toward my two-year-old brother's education—when he is ready. I am told to get a job as soon as I graduate.

"Why do you think you got the typewriter?" my mother asks.

Junior Achievement appeals more than ever as a good head start when the only skill I think I can bring to the workplace is an A+ in typing class.

Our Junior Achievement group meets once a week in the early evening in an empty office that is donated for that purpose. We are supplied with our product, a mini telephone that doubles as a bank, and a music box. They come in the cutest pastel colors. But before we can sell them, we have to first create a company. We brainstorm names. Decide on pricing. We learn how to draw up stock certificates to sell to our families and friends to raise money to manufacture our products. We craft bylaws on how our company is going to be run and elect officers. Our coaches are all experienced businesspeople who want to give back to the community and the next generation in particular. They share stories with us about what it was like to start out in different times, when they were our age and without mentors.

Once every year, two students from each group are chosen to attend a conference in Atlantic City, joining hundreds of other Junior Achievers from around the country. The night this year's recipients are to be selected, I am the only girl in attendance. It's explained to the group that one girl needs to be nominated to take part in a beauty pageant. So, along with the leading boy Achiever, I get a free trip to a hotel in Atlantic City for two days of workshops during the day and dances in the evening.

At the pageant, the other girls slowly sashay and strut around the ballroom. They look so pretty to me. I am ashamed of my body. When it's my turn, I hunch my shoulders, slouching down to hide my breasts and rush through my walk. In my head I curse what maturity has brought me, what my father does to me, and what I let boys do. But mostly I try to hide myself because we have to walk in front of everyone with the judges comparing who is the most beautiful to represent Junior Achievement to the whole country. I feel naked. I do not win as Miss Junior Achievement that year, and I did not expect to.

After the pageant I manage to skip the workshops and make out with one of the boys there. I feel free to be away from the restrictions at home.

Back in school, my favorite subjects are English literature, Spanish, dance, and biology. While thinking about what I might like to do after graduating, biology seems the most useful subject for getting a job. So I select the class in scientific drawing as an elective and meet Mr. Monopoli.

His kindness is boundless, and he helps me succeed when I possess zero artistic talent. He spends time each class ensuring that my work is good enough to meet the course requirements, touching up my sketches, giving me pointers for improvement. I spend almost the entire term on only two illustrations, one of the complex human digestive tract, in full color, in which I duplicate and label the organs, and the other of a sea bird in black and white. He takes pains guiding me through black feathering techniques. When he finds out that I have never been to a backyard barbecue, he invites me and four other girls from the class to his home in New Jersey.

There I learn that the Monopolis have no children of their own and relish our visits as their opportunity to be our surrogate parents. Mrs. Monopoli prepares trays of food in advance, feeding us hot dogs and burgers made on a grill and fresh Jersey-grown corn on the cob with melted butter. We even toast marshmallows on the fire after dinner. They talk to us like adults about our future direction after high school, about the care needed for dating and drinking. We listen more intently than to our own parents because of the respect they show us. And because it's apparent that they enjoy our company.

Barbeques at the Monopolis' become a Sunday routine during the entire summer vacation. We meet at school, cram into Mr. M's car, and cross the bridge into New Jersey for our afternoon of escape from the Bronx and our families' supervision. We help Mrs. M clean up afterwards, taking turns washing and drying the dishes, something we need to be ordered to do at home.

Two years have passed since I told Karen about my home life. So when Mr. Monopoli asks me why I am so down one day, I share that I'm having trouble at home and consider that maybe it's time to trust someone else with my secret.

"Come to my office at three," he offers, and I am grateful for the invitation. I can get this burden off my chest and get some help. This time I will be speaking to an adult with authority, not just another kid like me. He will know what to do. For a brief moment, I allow myself to imagine that he and Mrs. Monopoli will adopt me, getting me away from my parents at last.

I do notice when he locks the door behind me but am not overly concerned since we are going to talk about something private.

I look down at the floor even though I think of Mr. Monopoli as the good father/grandfather, and I tell him about my home situation.

The only question he asks when I am done is, "Who else have you told?"

"No one," I say. I'm unprepared for his question and horrified by what he does next. He unbuttons my blouse and puts his hand under my bra on my breast, and I freeze. Terrified, I think I have to get out of the office, but I cannot move. My legs feel as hard as iron bolted to the floor. What is wrong with me? This can't be happening. Why is it happening again? This is the last conscious thought I have before disappearing into no man's land and the chasing jaguar.

Chapter 9

Although he has never done this before, my Uncle Alan introduces me to a potential new client of his who just relocated from a small town called Gloversville in upstate New York. The town gets its name from an old factory built in the previous century where gloves are manufactured.

Bob Finkel is five years my senior and a manager at the Gimbels Department Store in the Roosevelt Field Mall on Long Island. I never shop there as prices are beyond my budget. Bob is a college graduate and owns a car too. My Uncle Alan doesn't know other young people to introduce him to, so he takes a chance with me, knowing that at seventeen, I am very mature for my age.

"Barbara, be a good girl and just do me a favor," Uncle Alan says to persuade me. "If it doesn't work out, you've at least done a good deed for someone new to the area." Cocking his head to one side, my uncle smiles his do-it-for-me smile that I can't resist. Then, too, Uncle Alan is married to my favorite Aunt Trudy, the one whose lipstick I try on whenever I visit their bathroom. I feel somewhat indebted to them. And dating someone who does not go to my high school and who owns a car does seem rather appealing.

Bob turns out to be a good boyfriend in the beginning. He buys me my first ever necklace, a small heart with a diamond at its center. He takes me to my senior prom and out for another first, an after-dinner club that features real live entertainers whom I know from American Bandstand. Paul and Paula's song is about true love and I visualize the lyrics changing to Bob and Barbara.

After four months of dating, Bob gets drafted at the same time as I start City College in the evenings and work as a clerical assistant in an insurance agency during the day. I need this job because my parents are now charging me room and board. Out of the thirty-three dollars I earn a week, they take fifteen dollars. But college is worth it. My mind is opened that first semester to different ways of thinking. Insightful questions get asked. "What did you think of Dr. King's 'I Have a Dream' speech on TV last month?" My peers are interested in what I think and say.

I love sitting on the lawn in between classes when it is light outside and meeting other students before the next class discussing politics, human rights, and philosophy. My freshman year also coincides with Vietnam, the summer of the Harlem Riots, the Civil Rights Act being signed into law, and the assassination of our beloved President Kennedy. He was the first president I wished I could have voted for when I turned eighteen. My reasons for wanting to vote for him may have been shallow. He represented the party I would register for as well as being young and handsome. But when he was killed, I felt both empty and angry. Empty because my hero was gone. And angry at anyone who could take a life. On campus, we hold each other and cry for the loss of our nation's hope. My education is happening outside of class on the green as well as indoors in a room.

Before he leaves for boot camp and deployment, Bob gives me what he calls an engagement gift, a gold watch with a star sapphire and diamonds on its cover. While I like getting gifts, I am more excited about starting college and do not consider the seriousness of his declaration. At about the same time, my parents announce that they are looking for a house on Long Island where my father is now working. The family will be moving soon. Because I am supposedly engaged, there will not be a room for me. But I don't see it the same way Bob does. In my mind engagement means that we will get married someday, but I'm not ready for that now. Since I started college,

FACING THE JAGUAR 75

my social circle has widened. I want to go to dances and date other boys. When I tell my parents a variation of this, my father forbids me to break up with Bob in a letter.

"He's serving his country. We're at war. Even if you and your conscientious objector friends don't believe in it, your country does. And you don't do that to a man." My father fires his warnings at me. "A Dear John letter is the worst thing you can do to a guy who's fighting for and preserving your freedom." Emphasis on *your*. "Date if you want to. Just don't let him know until he comes back."

So that's what I do. Unfortunately, when Bob returns after completing boot camp, his plans differ from mine.

"I was true to you while I was away," Bob starts as we sit side by side in the front seat of his car. "Being stationed in Texas, all the other guys had sex with Mexican prostitutes, but I didn't. Now it's time for you to deliver and prove your love."

"What do you mean?" I ask even though I think I know where this is heading. He has saved himself for me. "I'm not going to sleep with you, Bob." With a little remorse in my voice, I add, "I don't even want to be engaged anymore. And have been waiting all these months just to tell you face to face."

Before I can unlatch and take off the watch to return it to him, Bob's hand makes contact with my face.

I jump out of the car and run back to the apartment.

While my parents did not expect me to move to Long Island with them, that's what I do. I share a room with my sister and a household with my dysfunctional family once again.

The only person close to my age on Pearl Drive warns me about this Long Island social desert.

"Do you drive?" she asks. "No? Then you'll either end up dating married men like me or being very lonely." Monica seems very mature to me even though she tells me she is in her early twenties.

Her posture is lovely, and she speaks with confidence about the neighborhood, Long Island, and men in particular.

"I was innocent like you in the beginning," she warns. "Then I got wise."

Monica drives away down the block in her white Chevy Nova convertible, with its red leather interior, waving her hand back to me. "You'll see."

That's why when my father's new company needs a typist for the summer, I gladly go just to have something to do. There is one other young woman in the office named Fran. We talk about books and boys, music and movies. It makes going to work more fun.

One weekend, Fran gets into a serious car accident, leaving her in a full body cast with multiple broken bones and injured organs. The hospital she is sent to is located exactly one block from our new house.

When my father and his boss ask me to visit her on their behalf, I happily go see her. She is the only person my age I know, and I don't need a car to walk to Central General Hospital.

With a heavily exhaled cloud of smoke, my father blows at me before I leave, "Check on the flowers we sent her."

There is a floral arrangement from the Walters on Fran's night-stand. But the card is signed from Norma, Peter, Garry, Dennis, and Ringo. "Walters is a nice last name," I say, looking at Fran and smiling. "But who would name their kid Ringo?"

"Oh," she pauses, realizing something and then laughs. "You have the same last name as my friend from youth group at the synagogue. I'll have to introduce you. And Ringo is not a kid. He's a monkey. A group of boys I know have been coming to the hospital to visit ever since the accident. If you're here one time when they are, it'll be fun."

I'm not sure I want to meet a monkey owner, but I do want to meet a group of boys, especially ones who can drive to the hospital in their own cars.

FACING THE JAGUAR

* * *

Sure enough, on my next visit to Fran, three boys that she knows from youth group are there. There is Ira, a chubby, cherubic-looking guy; Garry, who is busy talking to the visitor for the patient in the bed next to Fran; and the one I am interested in, Harvey, the good-looking, sort of bad boy. He has the looks I am attracted to. His white T-shirt is rolled up at the shoulders, James Dean style, with a pack of Marlboros tucked under one side.

Ira and Harvey are busy catching Fran up with gossip from their youth group. Not knowing anyone they're talking about, I can't help but turn my attention to the patient in the next bed and her visitor. The visitor asks Garry if he has a car and can drive him home. I see by his shifting weight that Garry is uncomfortable, so on a whim, I interrupt.

"I thought you were going to take me home, Garry, to meet Ringo," I say, surprising both him and myself.

He looks at me, confused at first. Then it dawns on him. "Oh right. Sorry, guy." Garry turns to me and we both walk out into the hall.

"I only live a block away," I whisper. "I didn't want you to get cornered into doing favors for a complete stranger."

"Let's say goodbye to Fran and go," Garry suggests.

When we drive the one block to get to the house, Garry steps out of the car and accompanies me to the front door. I unlock it and turn to say goodbye, but he surprises me by walking inside and asking if I want to go to a movie. Not knowing what to do, I leave him sitting in the living room and go upstairs to talk to my mother.

"What should I do?" I hope she has some guidance for me this one time. "This strange guy I met at the hospital visiting Fran just walked into our house and wants to take me to a movie."

"Go," is all she says, returning to her book.

I don't know why I think she's good for any advice. Frustrated, I direct a snarky comment at her out of exasperation. "By the way, his last name is Walters and I'm going to marry him."

My life changes that night when Garry brings me home for the second time that day. We make out in the basement on a daybed we keep there for sleepover guests. I don't particularly like his kisses. They're wet and messy, but when he presses his body up against me, even through our two layers of clothing, my body begins to tremble. Starting at my toes and traveling up my legs all the way to my most private spot, opening and closing, muscles contracting and releasing tension and surprising me for the first time in my life. It is like an earthquake. I am euphoric and relaxed at the same time. These are feelings I've been afraid of for years. To not let them out when my father comes to me has had me holding them back for years. And releasing them now finally feels so good.

Being taught that my body exists to give pleasure to others, this moment of joy confirms my decision. Garry is a good person who is even willing to help a stranger. And look what he brings into my life. I *am* going to marry him.

Chapter 10

One of the first things I like about Garry Walters is his last name. In my limited social exposure at nineteen, I've worried about meeting a Jewish boy whose last name is Lipschitz or Fuchs, thinking about how the kids in school torment kids with such soundalike curse word names.

From the start, I believe Garry is a nice guy. Shortly after we meet, I experience his generosity firsthand when I need someone to come rescue me. After work one night, I walk the two miles home to change out of my dental assistant's uniform and catch a bus to Hicksville. Even though I hurry, I am left stranded at the Hicksville Long Island Railroad Station when the last westbound train of the evening departs just as I run up the platform stairs. That train would have only taken me to Jamaica, where I'd need to wait for another bus to travel to Queens College. I am tired just thinking about getting to class, then having to reverse the trip back.

I follow Dr. King's Selma march and President Johnson's signing of the Voting Rights Act this year from afar, but doing so makes me miss my earlier college experiences where I socialized and philosophized with like-minded peers. That just does not happen this late at night. I rush to school and back only to do homework and get ready to walk to work the next day. I am considering giving up on night school.

I don't know anyone else with a car who would come and get me this late, so I call Garry from a pay phone. He tells me he'll be there to pick me up in twenty minutes, and while I wait, his mother, Norma, stays on the phone with me.

"No girl should be alone at night in a dark train station," she says. "Stay on the phone with me until Garry gets there."

Too soon, I run out of change as the last coin drops. But there's a Dunkin' Donuts across the street, so I tell Norma I will wait inside where it's well-lit.

Garry picks me up and drives me back to meet his family that night. When we get there, I see that they have waited for us for dinner. It's their routine to all sit down as a family and catch up from the day. Norma is a big woman and welcomes me with an unusual greeting. "You are a little one. Aren't you? My bones weigh more than you do." She breaks out in a jovial smile, which I'm grateful for since I don't know how to respond to her comment.

Peter, Garry's father, is quiet but flashes his blue eyes almost flirtatiously at me. I am overwhelmed by this reception since I am crashing their evening. Dennis, Garry's younger brother, looks like his dad with light hair and eyes, the opposite of Garry's dark hair and eyes.

They're all curious about me and ask many questions:

"Where did you live before coming to Long Island?"

"What are you studying in school?"

"Do you have any sisters and brothers?"

"How do your parents feel about you traveling that distance at night and alone?"

Even though the questions come in rapid succession, I see that they're concerned for and curious about me. This is what it's like to be part of a normal, supportive family. I am learning about them at the same time.

The kitchen where we sit is decorated in glossy white wallpaper with bright yellow modern daisies scattered throughout. The window over the sink is topped with a valance in a matching fabric. Even the dinner plates are coordinated.

Norma makes dinner every night, whips up meals last minute from things like cans of soup and whatever happens to be in the extra freezer in the basement, fully packed to keep it running efficiently. There are Limoges and Wedgwood pieces as well as green plants all around the house, expanding from windowsills to end tables. Plush wall-to-wall carpet finishes pull the rooms together.

I learn that they're founding members of the synagogue they belong to, giving them the right to have the name, WALTERS FAMILY, engraved on brass plates throughout their entire front row of padded red velvet seats. These are seats of honor, I am told, since regular people have to sit on folding chairs in the extension room behind the sanctuary.

Norma has a cleaning lady, wears a mink stole, and drives a Cadillac. It's all very impressive to me since I live with my parents who expect half of my paycheck toward the expense of my room and board. Garry's father owns his own retail auto parts store and brings home enough money for them to own this split-level home on Long Island, a condo on an island in Florida, and a large cabana at a private beach club. To me it seems Garry lives a storybook life. His joy spills over to his love of animals. His house is filled with several fish tanks, a ring-tailed monkey in a zoo-sized cage, and one dog after another. I think anybody who is kind to animals must be a good person, especially having grown up in the housing projects where pets were prohibited. The only animals I saw daily were rodents scurrying from the landfill the projects were built on.

Garry is also a member of the Simian Society, a club of monkey owners who dress their pets in children's clothes or costumes and treat them like humans at monthly merry get-togethers.

On my second visit with the family, Norma asks me for a favor.

"When Peter and I go to Florida this winter, can we count on you to help Garry take care of the house and Ringo?"

The monkey is named after his ringtail, not the Beatles' drummer.

I'm not a fan of animals, but I'm on the spot with this woman who has been so nice to me. Besides, she only asks if I can help Garry. Not do it by myself.

"What's involved?"

"As far as Ringo is concerned," she explains, "you just have to make him breakfast." Then she quickly adds, "And bring in any mail or flyers left in the driveway. Plus water the plants."

"What's involved in Ringo's breakfast?" I ask meekly so as not to sound negative.

"Ringo's meal consists of two scrambled eggs, a quartered orange, and two slices of toast with cream cheese. Plus his vitamins."

Boy, this animal eats better than most humans, I think in amazement.

Ringo lives in the den, which is a long narrow room, one step down, on the opposite side of the house from the rest of the living quarters. It's the first room one comes to upon entering the house and furthest from the kitchen or bedrooms. I will soon start spending more time with Garry and learn that Ringo does not like sharing his attention. The monkey will screech, grab, and rattle the bars of the cage, throwing cedar chip shavings at us across the room until Garry goes and attends to him.

The first time I experience Ringo screaming and raging, I startle and turn quickly, whacking my elbow into Garry's nose. He's wearing a white crew neck sweater, and whether it's the blood or just my presence, it seems to send Ringo into a rant. He throws debris at me, even when I end up serving him his three-course breakfast. After Ringo's feeding time, Garry puts on a white aviator mechanic's uniform to clean Ringo's enormous cage.

I find Garry appealing in almost everything he does. He's attractive and has a good personality, always joking around, having fun with his friends. He reminds me of Fabian, my popular rock heart-throb. He even knows how to dance.

Early in our relationship Garry invites me to a youth group show he has a part in. The auditorium is large, and, not knowing anyone else, I sit alone. It gives me a lot of time to look around and compare what I see. Garry wears his hair in one of the favored styles of the day, trimmed close on the sides and back while leaving the hair on top slightly longer. He is dressed in a light blue crew neck sweater over a white button-down shirt open at the neck. His pants are shiny wool-and-silk-blend shark skin pegged in charcoal, fitted and tight with matching loafers. He dresses nothing like the greasers I know from the Bronx, and his role in the show is a dance scene. Something I wish I could do. Watching him dancing on stage with such confidence and style makes me feel like I am in the audience of *American Bandstand*. His lightness is a welcome change to my heavy life, to my heavy heart. To my shame.

All the childhood books I read and loved had happy families with working fathers and home-making mothers, lots of kids, and pets all living together in a big house. I want that so badly. I want a family and kindness and security. Garry represents all that—and he gives me the first orgasm of my life without sex. With our clothes on. I can't believe something like this is possible.

I was never able to give my fear a name before, but in fact I was terrified of something literally falling out between my legs during those times my father visited me at night. I held back any sensation, disappeared into the jungle, not wanting to give him anything in return. At least I think I held back any reaction. My body may have reacted uncontrollably to the stimuli from my father, but my mind went elsewhere, shielding me from any pleasure. After my experience with Garry, I know what I was holding in and holding back: an orgasm. And it feels so good, so wonderful not to hold back and to be able to find relief at last.

When it happens, we are in the basement of my parents' house. The space is more like a storage bin packed from floor to ceiling and filling every corner. There is extra furniture, like my grandmother's secretary bookcase, that hasn't found a home since we moved from the Bronx. Or the saggy old daybed with a red corduroy slipcover, which is the only place to sit. And my father's extra tools that are too big for the garage, as well as cartons of reject plastic shopping bags he manufactures with extra rolls of poly extrusion material. Then, too, there are mops and brooms and all sorts of cleaning supplies. The good news is that I feel sheltered and private with everything piled high surrounding us.

We start out kissing, but soon we're lying down face-to-face, body-to-body, on the daybed. Our bodies move in rhythm to our breathing until we are rubbing against each other. The more we rock and rub, the more I do not want to stop, to hold back what I feel coming. It falls out like a surprise. Waves of heat roll all the way to my toes until what I'd been afraid to lose bursts forth. My vagina is opening and closing, contracting and expanding, sending my body into spasms of private joy. At last, this is something for me, not just for the person who wants me. Up until this point, sex has been for them. Not me.

At nineteen, I am in love with my orgasm. It's a gift to release all the pressure, the tumescence that has been building up for years. And with Garry, it happens without penetration. Through two layers of clothing. Without any skin touching. Even better.

Right after Garry and I get engaged, Norma invites me to join her in preparing a holiday dinner where she will share one of the special recipes she is known for, homemade kreplach. These soup dumplings filled with ground meat and spices get eaten quickly in chicken soup but take a long time to make. The pockets of dough take the longest.

They need to be sealed so that the filling does not fall out in boiling soup.

While Norma prepares the dough, I am instructed to grind the meat to be used as filling. The grinder is an old-fashioned cranking, manual tool that attaches to the side of a kitchen counter, much like a vise on a tool bench. When the flour and eggs are being kneaded, Norma explains that it is new for her to have a girl around after raising two sons.

"I'm not used to girls," she starts off. "I had an older brother. But," her chest lifts then drops as she heaves a big sigh, "he died at two years old of meningitis when I was born."

I don't know how to react to this news but stop turning the grinder arm to look at her.

"My mother said that I required a lot of attention when they brought me home from the hospital and they failed to notice how sick he was. I always felt guilty that his death was my fault."

Norma is sharing more than her special recipe, and I listen intently to this woman who will be my new good mother.

"I spent my life making it up to my parents, doing everything they wanted until I met Peter."

As Norma rolls out the dough, she continues her story. "That was the only time I remember disappointing my parents. You see, Peter was married before. Plus, he was eighteen years older than me. My parents thought those two things were bad omens." She presses down hard with the wooden rolling pin, stretching the dough across the kitchen table.

Then Norma uses a sharp knife to cut the sheets of dough into two-inch squares. "Place a small amount of filling, around a half teaspoon, in the center of each square," she explains. "Then fold each square in half diagonally, dampen the sides with water, and pinch the edges closed."

This is painstakingly slow work since many of my dumplings

begin to open even before they hit the boiling water. I have to redo them many times. Her story keeps me trying to do a better job.

"They were against me marrying Peter, and I disobeyed them for the first time. A few months later, my father died. I was heartbroken. Here, let me show you how to pinch. You're too gentle."

Norma's fingers move so swiftly it is hard for me to follow. But I try to squeeze the dampened dough with more pressure.

"I was sitting shiva for my father when I discovered I was pregnant with Garry. Picture me on a hard cardboard box pregnant and non-stop crying. It should have been a happy time."

The boiling kreplach we finished fill the kitchen with the aroma of meat and onions as Norma continues her tale. "My mother died two months later. And there I was again, still pregnant, sitting on a box and crying. I believed this was my punishment for marrying against my parents' wishes."

I wonder if there is a message in there for me. But also think how horrible that must have been for her. First her brother's death, then losing both her parents. All I can muster is, "I'm so sorry."

"My parents never got to meet Garry, to be grandparents. I never got my chance to make them happy about my marriage to Peter."

I don't know what to make of her confession. And making kreplach is too much work for me. I file the recipe and the story away where I think neither will ever be used again.

My mother refuses to go shopping for my bridal gown.

"I never had a wedding of my own," she at least explains. "I need to find my own gown. It's my special day, too."

I stand frozen in place, stunned and not knowing where to go.

"You're leaving home. You want to be an adult. So be one," she says and leaves the room.

I save up two hundred dollars of my pay that I plan to use for the dress and my trousseau. The only female role model I can think of with good taste to guide me is Jackie Kennedy. I buy a cream-colored sheath with a little pill box and a short veil. Cream because I am uncomfortable wearing pure white since I am not a virgin. And the simplest outfit because I equate getting married with a sign of my sophistication.

Norma calls me one day when I am at work in the dental office.

"I need you come over right away," she says breathlessly. "How soon can you get here?"

I am surprised to hear from her and can't just leave in the middle of the day. "Maybe you should call Garry or Peter?" I suggest. "They can get to you faster."

"No. It's a woman thing. I need you."

I promise her I'll get there as soon as I can. When I tell my boss, the doctor, about the call, he's reassuring. "Go," he says. "Your future mother-in-law is a priority right now."

When I get to the house, the front door is ajar. As I step into the foyer, I call out her name.

"I'm up here in the bedroom," comes the answer.

When I reach the master bedroom, Norma is sitting on the bed in her nightgown motioning for me to come in.

I am scared to help someone I do not know well, but I feel valued at the same time. Without daughters, who else could she count on for help?

"Sit here, dear," she says, pointing to the floor beside her bed. "This is where the boys sit when they come home from a date." She pauses before adding, "They tell me everything. I mean, everything."

I am not happy to hear that Garry may be telling his mother about the private things we do when alone, but I am more concerned about what this has to do with her needing me to get over there so quickly.

Not wanting to appear rude, I wait for her to tell me.

She hands me a piece of paper. It is a letter from the draft board. Garry's number has come up.

"I need you to secretly get married tonight. Then to become pregnant immediately. Your parents can continue with the wedding plans and don't have to know."

I am dumbfounded. Sure, I am against the war in Vietnam, but I'm also patriotic. When your country calls, you answer.

"My father served in the army," I tell her, starting to explain my position.

"I don't think you understand," Norma interrupts before I can say anything else. "See that shoebox." She points to the shelf at the top of her open closet. "In it you will find a gun. If you don't get married quickly, I'll be forced to shoot one of Garry's toes off. That's how much I love him."

Chapter 11

We do not elope as Norma wanted, but we do move the date of our wedding up by five months. Garry ends up getting an occupational deferment when he lands a job at Grumman Aerospace as a weights analyst recording the weight for parts of a jet plane used in Vietnam. Neither the draft nor a lost toe is a concern any longer.

Our wedding takes place in a large catering hall. Catering mill might be a more appropriate name. It's the type of business with multiple ballrooms on multiple floors. Sliding partitions separate each room with adjustable walls depending on the size of the party. Not soundproof, music can be heard competing with the different tastes of each party. You might have reggae out blasting a polka or tarantella. The gigantic crystal chandeliers vibrate, adding to the cacophony from overhead.

People are wandering past me in a steady flow. They might be looking for their assigned ballroom. They might be in search of the matron-assisted powder rooms. Or, they might be shoppers accompanied by a sales representative checking out the facility for a future event of their own. You can always tell this last group because they are dressed too casually for the occasion.

Also in the lobby that day are both sets of our parents, who get into a huge fight. Having the same last name causes problems with the photographer. It starts when he asks for Mr. Walters to be in a picture with the bride and my father shows up. Insulted to be put aside because of a mistake, my father argues with him, insisting that *he* is Mr. Walters. Passersby stop and stare. Voices get louder as they try to out-shout each other. When my father won't relent, won't stop causing a scene, Garry's parents tell the photographer, who was hired by them to provide individual photo albums and a movie of the wedding, to hand *Mr. Walters* the bill. And making a hand washing motion, walk away.

At the same time on the day of our wedding, something unexpected but not unwelcome happens. After the ceremony, we are in a common lobby area taking dozens of posed group shots. We start with the immediate family and continue to the most extended relatives on both sides. I am in almost every photo and end up standing around for a long time while someone tries to retrieve the missing members who are getting drunk or gorging themselves on baby lamb chops or pigs-in-blankets.

Standing still for so long in my wedding dress and heels, I feel lightheaded and empty bellied. I don't want to sit and crease my gown. I start to sway holding the heavy, oversized bouquet Garry's family has gifted me for the day, when I suddenly hear the sound of a heavy metal dungeon door clang shut and reverberate, first very loudly, then lower and softer, echoing until it seems to close shut. The noise resounds for almost a minute. I look around to see if anyone else has heard it. No one is paying attention. So I interpret it as a private message to me announcing the finality of something. Maybe my move to freedom. I feel even lighter, liberated from the prison I have been in for my entire life and believe in that moment nothing can harm me ever again. I remind myself, *I am going home to my first ever home of my own, my castle.* There is a moat surrounding the castle where I will live happily ever after. Garry and his family. My new family of choice will protect me.

Of course, I do not know what marriage really is, especially based on the experience my parents provided. I hold a lot of fantasies around romantic love, though, from the novels I've read, and I look forward to playing house. Ruffled curtains and China dinnerware. I am free of my parents, especially my father, and I feel untangled and untouched by my troubled past.

Add into that mix all the Harlequin Romance books I now read. One of the writing magazines says it's the easiest place ever for new authors to get published, with every book following the same basic formula. I just have to use my imagination to fill in the blanks. All my dreams are coming true. No more parents. A husband to love me. Becoming a writer. A home of my own. While I have not discussed it yet with Garry, I'm certain I'll have plenty of time to write. Garry has just bought me a Chevy Corvair. No more walking back and forth to work.

In this naïve fantasy mindset, I am surprised when married life shows up with constant unexpected revelations and two big bombshells almost immediately.

The first is about my sister, Rhonda. When my parents go on vacation, what my mother calls "the overdue honeymoon we never had," they ask me to drive by their house to check on things while they are away. They really mean check on my sister. And since Garry and I did not plan a honeymoon due to his mother changing his college major three times and having classes the next day, we are available.

On the night we go visit her, we drive past the house to find all the lights on and the front door wide open. Walking through the house calling my sister's name produces no response, as there is also loud music coming from somewhere. We walk through every room on the first and second floors of the house. With my heart pounding, I at last reach my parents' bedroom, which is the furthest room on the third floor. This is a room I have stayed away from and never feel physically comfortable entering. There on their marital bed is my sixteen-year-old sister, undressed and bouncing up and down on top of some guy to a wild rhythm and beat. The headboard is pounding and harmonizing with both the loud rock music and the creaking springs.

"Rhonda!" I scream, not knowing what else to say. She stops for a moment and continues as though we aren't there. "How can you do this in their bed?" is all I can think of to ask.

She doesn't even stop bouncing and just laughs. "If our father can fuck me," she says, her body rising and falling, "I can fuck anyone I like." The boy underneath her is unfazed and just accepts her continuous momentum. Doesn't he care what she just said? "In his bed!" she shouts back. "It's poetic!" She's laughing hysterically at her own joke as she turns back to her partner.

I almost fall backward down the steps, dumbfounded by both her response and revelation. I fumble with my pathetic retort. "Well at least you could have the good sense to close the front door and turn off the lights. Or else anyone can walk in here like this is Grand Central Station."

Turning around to leave, I find Garry standing there. His face is scrunched up as though he smells something rancid when I realize I have a bigger problem. I have never told him about my father, so how am I going to explain it now? I decide to explain everything quickly as I don't have much of a choice at his point.

We get back into the car in silence. On the way home, he lets me know what he thinks of me now that he knows: "You're used baggage." His reaction shocks me but not as much as finding out that I unconsciously passed the problem of my father onto my sister. "I got used baggage," he says again, apparently feeling sorry for himself. "My mother told me you were no good. That the apple doesn't fall far from the tree." He's sad and disappointed, like he's the victim in this situation.

Fighting with Garry or insisting that I'm not used baggage or even worrying about my future is not where my mind is right now. I have a more immediate need. I have to do something about getting my sister out of that house.

"Who can we go to for help protecting my sister?" I ask, thinking out loud, already knowing Garry will not have an answer. "We can go to the police. No, we can't," I answer myself. "We can call one of my relatives. No, we can't do that either." All these actions risk bringing down my father's wrath. And who knows what that would mean. "We can . . . we . . . can . . . we can go to the rabbi." In my agitation, I can't see other options or know of anyone else who might be able to help.

Rabbi Spielman officiated at both Garry's bar mitzvah and our wedding. As an adult, I think of rabbis as wise and learned men, offering guidance and support, dedicated to their flock. Examples of the highest human values.

I call Rabbi Spielman early the next morning. When he hears the panic, my nearly hysterical voice over the phone, he says to come right in.

He sits in his office behind a wooden desk cluttered with papers and offers us the two armchairs facing it. "What's wrong?" he asks. "You haven't been married long enough to have big problems," he adds with a chuckle.

Rabbi Spielman seems larger in his office than on the pulpit. Up close I can see how wide he is and how frightening his dark black hair and beard are. Without his white clerical robes, he looks almost ominous. But I remind myself that he was pleasant enough preparing for our ceremony. Always one to drone on and be repetitive when delivering his sermon, I am surprised that he gets right to our reason for visiting him.

I struggle with where to start and how much to reveal. I am frozen in thought and can hear my heart thumping rapidly, forcing me to hurry up. "I need to adopt my sister," I suddenly blurt out. "And get her out of my parents' house." I pause to catch my breath for a moment and organize my thoughts, then explain, "My father is having sex with her." There, I said it. Even though this is the third time I've spoken about my father, it does not get easier.

The rabbi's expression goes from inviting to incredulous as his dark eyebrows furrow and his jaw tightens, squaring off. He presses his fingertips together in the shape of a spire and holds the tips to his lips, leaning his elbows forward on the desk, obviously thinking before he responds.

"That's not possible," he finally concludes, shaking his head up and down as though he agrees with this declaration. "A Jewish father would never do anything like that. Your sister must be making up a story. Teenage girls sometimes do that to gain attention."

"Rabbi," I plead. "She's not making it up. He did it to me. So I know that it's real."

Now the rabbi puts his hand on his chin, massaging his beard, then covers his lips while he thinks for a moment before responding again. "I'm sorry to say this, Barbara, but you must have misinterpreted your father's actions. You must have wrongfully thought his loving affection was sex."

Feeling blood rush up my neck, swelling and tightening my throat, I want to choke this man. To make him feel the way he just made me feel. I am so angry. What kind of spiritual leader is he? "I'm a married woman now, Rabbi. As you know," I stress for emphasis. "I am not misinterpreting loving affection for sex. I know the difference." I stand firm, and I don't even feel badly for shouting at a rabbi.

He keeps his calm but doesn't engage me any further. He simply stands and heads for the door to dismiss us, saying, "I'm sorry I can't help you. A Jewish father would never do something like that." He's convincing no one but himself.

When I stand to leave, Garry, who has said nothing during this meeting, stands as well. He looks at Rabbi Spielman and shrugs his shoulders as though he doesn't know what to do with me. I feel as violated as I did when Mr. Monopoli opened my blouse back in high school. I do not have time in that moment to think that all men might stick together. Or that incest is so terrible that people, even professional clergy, would rather deny its existence than have to deal with it. I have to get help for my sister on my own.

After that night at my parents' house and the revelation about my sister, the routines and roles of our marriage are permanently changed. Garry begins treating me differently. Or maybe being in such a heightened state of anxiety and consciousness, I am noticing his behavior for the first time. He used to be gentle and giving, but now it's like a beast has been unleashed in him. This is a beast that feels vaguely familiar, frightening, and immobilizing. Leaving me with another problem I feel unequipped to handle.

His habit of taking care of himself sexually becomes ritualistic, at least several times each night. After he finishes, he throws his dirty clothes under the bed for me to clean up as a reminder that I am dirty too. They join stacks of dirty dishes from the snacks he takes into the bedroom. Our lovemaking turns purely physical. When he is done, he empties his pockets of change, leaving the coins on my dresser as my weekly allowance. It is not enough to live on and it's insulting. I guess that's his point. I am used baggage and don't deserve anything more. He feels misled and burdened too.

I offer to get another job in addition to working in the dental office as a way to bring in more money. "If a man's wife works, it's a sign he's a poor provider," he tells me. Garry has adopted his father's old-fashioned philosophy, though it doesn't make sense in current times or in our lives. "But you can volunteer at the synagogue or Hadassah," he concedes. I am not ready and probably never will be ready to go work with Rabbi Spielman. And my mother-in-law, who's now openly telling me I did not fall too far from the tree, is a lifetime Hadassah member. That is enough to keep me away for life. I don't know what words Garry used to tell his parents about my history. But since he calls me used baggage and a burden, it can't be good. I am uncomfortable whenever I see them now. They mostly ignore me and say snide remarks about my family. If I think about it, I become more anxious.

Over the next few weeks, my focus is still on getting my sister away from my parents' hell. Not easy to do without any help or financial resources. That's when my research leads me to Jewish Community Services and their sliding payment scale, based on ability to pay.

Meeting the counselor at my first appointment is an immediate relief. A woman. She's petite in stature and looks like she could be related to my Grandma Walters. I trust her to help. I allow myself to believe she'll be someone who will believe me and understand. She asks what brings me in today and listens with care and concern on her face. I am floored when she echoes Rabbi Spielman's bottom line: "Jewish fathers don't do that. You must be mistaken."

"Where does that leave me?" I ask, desperation in my voice. "My Jewish father did."

Her response hurts and reopens wounds from some of the most painful parts of my childhood. "You have a vivid imagination, dear." She pushes up her glasses and turns the pages of her desk calendar. "I would be glad to set up your next appointment for counseling. We can concentrate on putting that imagination of yours to better use."

Doing what? I wonder. I leave without looking back. Denying my father's behavior and how it affects me daily, compounded with the guilt and shame I feel now that I know he's hurting my sister, my lack of confidence and self-respect to fight back, my confusing sex for love, and my poor choice of a life mate. It's all a messy swirl that leaves me feeling more hopeless than I imagined possible when I dared to dream of a new and better future.

Chapter 12

My sister's behavior goes into overdrive after the run-in in our parents' bedroom. I am unable to protect her by getting custody. She solves the problem by herself, leaving home and getting married shortly thereafter.

I am not happy about how things worked out. I feel guilty about passing the problem of my father onto Rhonda, of being too fearful to have confronted it myself. Or too naïve thinking it was over when I left. Then, too, is the fallout with Garry and his family, and how they're now treating me as though I am the problem. No one expresses concern or compassion for what happened to me, except for Karen. For the rest of my life, any time I've told, I've been left with a hollow, soulless feeling inside of me. Each time I speak up, it seems it's another failed attempt to find my voice. I am left wondering what is wrong with me again and again. I am not believed. I am a bad person. Even authorities deny my experience.

In spite of his change in behavior, one benefit of being married to Garry is that I have space and autonomy. He starts working two jobs and doesn't want much input on household decisions. With a singular exception: Garry will follow in his parents' footsteps, insisting that I be a stay-at-home mom.

"When the day comes that we have a child," he announces, "you cannot work outside the house." The idea that a working woman makes it look like her husband's not a good provider is indicative of an earlier era.

Throughout my childhood, my most favorite times were when I was alone in our apartment, with no criticism, no beatings, no violations. When Garry asks that I comply, staying home does not seem like it will be a hardship. So even before we have a child, with Garry's two jobs, I still manage sacred alone time. It feels like freedom. I don't know what I am doing in making household decisions like what towels to buy or how to cook a chicken. But apparently I am ballsy, ignorant, or observant enough to take a stab at it and learn from the mistakes.

We had been unable to sign a long-term lease before the wedding because of Garry's 1-A draft status and not knowing where he could be sent. To start our life together, we end up renting a two-room furnished apartment in the dormer of a small cape cod house, which requires us to climb up a long flight of stairs to reach our quarters.

The back room is set up as a bedroom. The sloped ceiling that the head of the bed rests against means we cannot sit up without bumping our heads. The front room serves as a living room and the only eating area, as well as access to the staircase down to the street. The small walkway in between the rooms houses a utility table, serving as a counter with an electric double hot plate on top and a small refrigerator underneath, as well as the door to the bathroom. Dishes and pots are washed in the bathroom sink or bathtub, depending on their size.

Finally, after being married for six months, which feels like a lifetime, the deferment becomes official. We find a cute three-room garden apartment nearby on the ground floor next to a railroad track. Each time an express train flies past, everything hanging on the walls also travels, vibrates, rattles, and shakes. This requires someone to go around and straighten everything back to their original positions about once an hour during peak traffic times. But the good news is that we now have an eat-in kitchen with a full-sized sink, refrigerator, and stove, in addition to a shared laundry room in the building. The thought of not having to drag our wash to a public laundry is an extra benefit and very appealing since I have to do our wash at night after work and dinner. The public laundromats I'd been using for the past six months attracted some very sketchy-looking people at night. Being a young woman there alone after dark, especially when folding my undergarments, was unsettling on more than one occasion.

I invest myself in decorating our new apartment and learning from my peers. This year, 1967, is a year of avocado green décor with upholstery blended in shades of deep blue brocade fabrics. I like the textured, raised tapestry look of multicolored patterns and loose sofa pillows. Newlyweds that year are buying dark Mediterranean-styled furniture built from heavily carved wooden frames. All my friends have their homes decorated even before they get married. So once again, I am playing catch-up.

"It'll always look messy with loose cushions," Norma warns me. *It'll look uptight and uncomfortable with a solid straight-back cushion like she has*, I think.

For our wedding, she gifted us the furniture for our apartment, which seemed very generous at the time but has also meant I'm subjected to her opinions and her having more say in what gets chosen. I begin to resent her ability to use money to dominate our lives. It becomes a constant battle over even the smallest of details, with her reminding me that she has experience. And that I've learned from what she calls "trash."

Imagine my surprise, coming home from work early one day, to find her and two of her friends in our bedroom. I catch them mid-tour.

"How do you like the bed I bought for Garry?" The bed that was still unmade from that morning when I left for work. And the kitchen sink still full of last night's dinner dishes too.

Garry had given his mother a key for emergencies, which in her case meant potty stops due to her weak bladder. I could not tell if this was one of those occasions, but I doubted it given the presence of her friends. All I felt was humiliation. Then anger.

* * *

With no experience in being a homemaker beyond vacuuming and dusting, never seeing my mother do any housework, I live in a fantasy world of what I imagine normal family life is like. I pay careful attention to what my friends do, and everyone else's choices become my constant blueprint. Our bed and our dishes are now done immediately upon finishing or rising every day to ward off any future surprise visits, critical eyes, or mother-in-laws with weak bladders.

Starting our family is another challenge. My friends become pregnant apparently the first time they look at each other, even without much trying. Jealous, I feel as though it is not happening fast enough for me. Every month when I get my period, I cry just like I did the first time I menstruated when I thought I had cut myself. After twelve months of not succeeding, I am crushed, crying from a sense of overwhelming disappointment and failure. This is another way something is wrong with me. I must be to blame. I am accustomed to taking too much responsibility on myself. I am used to being criticized unjustly. This time is no different. Except I am doing it to myself.

I become obsessed with succeeding by taking my temperature daily. Watching for ovulation signs. Holding my legs in the air for half an hour after intercourse. Charting the ups and downs. I confide my disappointment to a few friends who tell me, "It's only been a year," or "It will happen."

Soon, my friends stop telling me when they become pregnant, knowing it will hurt my feelings due to how sensitive I am about the subject. I watch their growing bellies, their maternity clothes, their painted nurseries, and go home and cry myself to sleep.

Finally, a year and a half into my marriage, I become pregnant. Switching gears, I believe my life is set forever. When I tell Garry, he is nowhere near as happy as I am. Suddenly, he seems nervous, realizing that we are actually going to become parents and looking like he wishes he could take it back.

"Boy, that was fast," he says, exhaling the words, breathy and loud. "I don't know anything about babies," he continues after a moment, shaking his head. "You want this more than me. You'll have to do everything yourself." And as an afterthought, "I won't change diapers."

I recognize what is happening right away. "Not to worry. I do have a lot of experience from being around and helping with Rob," I reassure him. Rob is now just six years old, and I regularly changed diapers, sanitized bottles, fed and burped him. *I'm used to doing everything around here anyway*, I think. "You have enough to think about with your two jobs. And loads of experience taking care of Ringo and Brandy," I wisely add. Garry's mood lifts when I mention his two favorite pets, the ring-tailed monkey and the cocker spaniel he left with his parents when we got married.

Pregnancy is my way out of failure. I succeed at something. This will be the first grandchild on both sides of our families. This child will hold a special place of honor. And, as the child's mother, I can fill my role and play house. I'm hoping, too, that Norma will think more highly of me. That by continuing the family line, I will earn some respect from her.

According to the obstetrician, our baby's due date is January 29, 1968. We put off a lot of the work and are unprepared for Adam's entry into the world on Christmas Day in 1967, when I start labor. Not knowing what to expect, I don't recognize the nausea and back twinges that have bothered me all that day and night as labor. The only relief I get from not being able to sleep is squatting in front of the stove and scouring the bottom broiler until it looks new again, all shiny blue with bright white dots. Then hunching over the bathtub, turning my energy to the discolored grout between the tub and tile.

I also do not know what to expect from childbirth itself, thinking if women gave birth for centuries in the fields where they worked, my job would be a lot easier in a hospital with a doctor. If there was a doctor attending, I would not remember him later. I would only remember the nurses who took care of me. First, I am given an enema and an IV. Two new experiences for me. Next my pubic area is slathered with iodine before being shaved. All of this is embarrassing. Then I am informed that my water is going to be broken.

"What will I do when my water is broken?" I ask in wonder.

A nurse presses her chin down, giving me a knowing look over the top of her glasses and laughs before answering, "You're going to lay there in it."

My last thought as I feel myself going under is, *How is that possible?* In the next moment a warm gush of liquid flows out of my body, settling at my bottom until it seems to engulf all of me from my toes to my upper back. I close my eyes and laugh to myself because the nurse is right.

When I awaken, I'm alone in a narrow room. There is no one there to talk to. No husband, family, baby, or even a roommate. I am still in a hospital gown and very sore between my legs, afraid to get up and walk to ask questions, feeling like something could fall out of me if I stand.

Later that day, Garry and my in-laws come to visit and have already seen the baby through the nursery window. They tell me it's a boy. It does not seem right that visitors meet Adam before I do. I make a promise to myself: *This will never happen to me again.* I will not allow myself to be put to sleep and miss the experience of bringing my baby into the world. Now, because it is visiting hours at the hospital, they won't even bring my baby to me. Only when all visitors go home for the night is Adam brought into my room and put into my arms.

Even though I was fourteen years old when my brother was born, I didn't remember Rob being as small as Adam, who is born a month early. My brother also remained in the hospital for five days before I ever saw him. When I unwrap Adam's blanket to examine his body, he's all red, wrinkly, and scaly, like he has raw, bumpy chicken skin. Not what I expect looking at pictures of the babies on the Gerber Baby Food jars. No plump, round rosy cheeks for him.

Even though Adam loses a few ounces while in the hospital, he manages to weigh five pounds and can go home. Every day his rough skin evens out, becomes pinker as I stand over his crib or lay down with him on our king-sized bed, watching him for hours. As my child fills out, he fills me with wonder and a love I have never known possible. For every disappointment in my life, this is the time that far exceeds any imagination or fantasy I have conjured up. Adam is a beautiful, perfect piece of me. And of course, Garry too. Somehow, I feel like I have done this all by myself, from the temperature taking to the pregnancy to the post-partum daily baby care and the nighttime feedings. I begin to think that maybe I'm not such a loser after all. Here is something I can do well. Be a good mother.

I spend my days marveling at Adam's self-regulation. He knows when to move, to utter sounds, to change expressions, even when to sleep. We go for walks every day in the huge Coach carriage Norma has bought for him. Some days we have no destination except to get out of the apartment for fresh air. My mother-in-law chose this impractical carriage for Adam because it was what she used to stroll down Kings Highway in Brooklyn twenty-five years ago with Garry. Showing him off for the neighbors, she said. The wheels are huge and its body is metal and heavy to lift. A lighter fabric, in a smaller size that I could fit into the back seat of the car for our doctor visits, would make more sense.

By Adam's first birthday, the big space our apartment originally offered is now filled with a crib, changing table, highchair, playpen, as well as the Coach carriage. Luckily, a two-bedroom apartment becomes available and we grab it. With the move, Adam gets his own room. This will be the first time we are all not sleeping in the same room together.

Once again, Norma furnishes our apartment. This time with a giant four-foot stuffed bear, a train set, a wooden rocking horse, a 250-piece set of multisized wooden blocks, and a pull-along xylophone. I feel like she is stealing the joy I have in being Adam's mother. I want to be the one who introduces him to new experiences. It feels like she is trying to be the good mother, leaving nothing for me to give him. While Norma does not cut me any slack about my family, she is very proud of her grandchild and boasts about him to anyone who will listen. I take some pride in that.

I give him all my time. With Garry working both his day job and at his father's auto parts store evenings and weekends, Adam and I are alone a lot. After breakfast, Adam plays in his playpen while I make the beds and vacuum. I then take him out of the playpen and join him on the floor, building skyscrapers and knocking them down or making music on the xylophone. He prefers the pots, pans, and covers under the kitchen cabinet, which he bangs on with wooden spoons. When he is able to safely roam the apartment, he gravitates to this cabinet and takes out his instruments. I turn the radio on for him to a popular music station and he accompanies the artists with his unique percussive rhythms.

In awe of how perfect Adam is, I can't help but wonder if I might have been the same way as a baby. I know my purpose now. I have so much love to give. I love being a mother and parenting Adam. For the moment, all seems right in the world.

Chapter 13

Because of the difficulty I had conceiving the first time, my gynecologist suggests I begin trying the year after Adam is born. This way, if it takes another year and a half to conceive, the children will end up with the ideal age difference according to child experts in the early '70s. It does take even longer than that, but finally, we are pregnant again.

To help Adam adjust to a new sibling, we enroll him in a nursery program for two hours a day, three times a week. This is where I meet other young mothers and make some new friends. The nursery program is a cooperative one requiring at least one parent to volunteer and be present every other week. Of course, that responsibility falls to me, but it also gives me a chance to see my child compared to his peers. Adam is quick and bright, memorizing lyrics to popular and childhood songs. But what's most amazing is his ability to put together a jigsaw puzzle upside down and backward, having only the gray felt paper backing as a guide. No colors, no pictures. Even Mrs. Marx, Adam's nursery schoolteacher, says she never encountered anything like this in all the years she has been teaching.

Lindsay comes into the world very differently than Adam. I have false labor for two weeks before she is born. Going to the hospital the two extra times I am not ready is embarrassing and humiliating. "You should know better, Mother," the nurses say. "This is not your first." Perhaps because Adam was born a month early with barely any pain, I am unprepared for going past my due date with this second delivery. I overeat at a card party on the night before Lindsay's birth, and when I finally arrive at the hospital in real labor, there's nothing to be done. No shaving. No anesthesia. No waiting. Just birth. This is what I said I wanted the first time. And now I have a boy and a girl. The perfect family. I want for nothing else. And because it is the middle of the night, it is not visiting hours. Lindsay comes to me right away.

Lindsay is beautiful with a flawless round face and wide, round eyes. She is an extremely physical baby. Our baby nurse (a gift from Norma) is as amazed as I am when she flips over on her changing table from her back to her stomach at three days old.

At eight months old, when she toes in, the orthopedist attaches a bar to a pair of stiff shoes to realign both her legs. This will support her leg bones to develop and form correctly without turning in while allowing her ankles to be flexible. She needs to wear this apparatus as much as possible, including while sleeping. Even with this metal attachment, held through the soles with screws and bolts, Lindsay begins walking at eight months, holding her feet in the correct position. Hobbling along and balancing would be more descriptive and accurate of her gait. Nothing stops her.

On her first birthday, Lindsay climbs out of her crib, apparently in an attempt to pull down a picture of Jack and Jill off the wall, banging her face with the corner of the frame. Bleeding from her forehead into her eye, she navigates down the stairs until she can get my attention.

I am in the kitchen getting ready for her first birthday party, putting finishing touches on the homemade potato salad I prepared to accompany the barbecue, when she enters the room in her diaper, her orthopedic apparatus, and her torso covered in blood.

I freeze before my maternal instinct kicks in. Grabbing the nearest dishtowel, I press it next to her eye where the blood is still spurting from. I pick my baby up and run to my car. I drive all the way to the emergency room with only one hand, using the other to compress the wound over her eye.

The emergency room is active when we arrive. Almost every seat is taken by people waiting to be seen. I'm dressed for the party, in full makeup and wearing a new sundress I bought for the occasion. I head directly to the admissions window and ask for help. When the nurse sees all the blood, she comes from around her desk and takes the baby from me.

"What happened?" she asks, rushing Lindsay into a partitioned section, pulling a curtain around us. "Moth-ther?" she adds, stretching the word out toward the end and giving me a questioning look.

I don't really know and Lindsay can't tell us. But I can tell the nurse is scrutinizing me, staring too long in my direction. That's when it hits me. I am dressed for a party while my baby is in a soiled diaper with a bloodied dish towel and her orthopedic apparatus as her accessories for the day.

"I know what this might look like." I am suddenly reminded of my mother who preened and took great care of her appearance and neglected mine. Feeling guilty, I start to explain just as a doctor walks in. "Today is her first birthday party. I used her naptime to get myself ready. All her pretty things were laid out for when she got up. Except . . ." Before I can finish, Lindsay is standing up on the examining table showing off her stance.

"You've got an active one here, Mother," the doctor says in a kindly voice and a wink to the nurse. "Since she has a party when you get home, instead of stitches, why don't I give her a butterfly bandage? Less chance of scarring and she'll look better in the pictures."

I spend the next year constantly being distracted from my chores or our schedule looking for where Lindsay may have gone to, both inside and outside the house. We don't know to call her behavior hyperactive. She's so unlike her older brother, who sat in his playpen for hours fitting shapes into openings or building tall towers, content to be by himself. One time I finally find her hiding in the clothes dryer, peering out of the round window at me after I frantically searched all around in other spots. Another time, after loading groceries into the back seat of the car and turning momentarily to push the shopping cart away, I look back to find myself locked out of the car. Lindsay has depressed the door lock button.

I plead with her to unlock the door. "Please pull up the button," I cry while she ignores me. "Mommy needs to get in."

My words serve no purpose. Lindsay has her own plans. She just sits there, content and strapped into her child safety seat, pulling groceries from the bags. Ultimately, I ask someone from the crowd gathering around us to call the police, who try to charm her with a lollipop when they get there. Unsuccessful with that tactic, they use their Slim Jim tool to pry open the window.

I hear about a women's empowerment group from some of the mothers at the nursery school. The course description sounds right up my alley. Parenting two children basically alone with an absent and punishing partner leaves me feeling powerless.

Garry seems to spend more time away from home these days, leaving me to manage both children's needs. When I ask for help, he says, "I'm the breadwinner. House and kids are your job."

The group meets once a week for a sharing circle that's facilitated by a female psychologist. She talks about the women's liberation movement. About how men are not superior to women. About how we do not need to be subordinate to them. I sense that everything Cynthia says is right and think about how it relates to Garry and me.

At one of our first meetings, Cynthia instructs the group to write a letter to our five-year-old self. She guides us through a visualization. We close our eyes and picture ourselves sitting in front of the house we lived in at that age. It's our job to tell our child self what kind of things will be happening in our life over the next twenty years and write that message to help prepare them. When we are done, Cynthia goes around the circle asking each of us to share. My letter is unlike the others.

Most of the women talk about pretty party dresses and hair bows. Loving parents and summer camp. Sweet sixteen parties and going away to college. Some travel through Europe meeting new people before finding husbands. My letter is full of love for little me, but I also tell her that some bad things will happen to her. I feel her inside me and cry both for her and with her for the first time in my life. Two of the other women in the group cry along with me. Cynthia talks to me after the session and offers to work with me privately.

Around this time, Rhonda starts pressuring me to meet with our father. She's on a mission to find out whether he knows how much he has hurt us and to confront him about the lasting effects of what she calls "his lousy parenting."

The old childhood fear of my father killing me becomes obsessive. I picture the guns, his strength and force, the pain of being shot, even imagine a bullet entering my body and exploding inside me. I carry a lot of guilt at being the older sister and at not having stopped my father, leaving the problem of his assaults for my sister to deal with after I got out of the house. Especially after the letter to my little self. So, while I don't want to confront our father, I feel like I owe it to Rhonda to do so. I also feel sick to my stomach about agreeing to do something I so strongly don't want to do.

I get nauseous thinking about what I am committing to and struggle to eat or sleep. I barely take care of myself or my children for days in anticipation of being shot. I write love letters to my kids in case anything were to happen. I think about suicide. About the ways available to me. I have no access to pills. I can cut my wrists but dread feeling any more pain. The only source I deem reasonable and available is gas. I feel I'm losing control of my life. I believe I have the same mental illness as my father who did not know right from wrong. Without understanding how he could hurt us so much, I guess that he is mentally unwell, definitely mentally unstable. And that's what I feel like right now.

I do not want my children to inherit this disease that runs in my family. I imagine they will be much better off without me in the picture.

Garry and I start getting invited to parties in other couples' homes at the height of my anxious state. I can hardly put myself together while the other women come dressed to impress. Looking ready for the runway. Very coordinated and sexy. There is an abundance of alcohol, pot, and quaaludes at these parties, and quickly the conversation turns to sex and extramarital affairs. I try hard not to be different because I think this is a chance to be part of the "in" crowd. While no sex happens at the parties, the genders separate and talk about it. I find out from Garry that the men talk about going to strip bars with back rooms for lap dances and hand jobs. They share French porn films. That's when I discover that Garry has the largest collection of adult Betamax cassettes, which he keeps covered on the top shelf of our hall coat closet and freely dispenses among the men.

The women talk about how their husbands are unfaithful and that they're okay with it because they have everything and more: gifts of jewelry born of guilt.

At that year's New Year's Eve party, the other women come wearing gold and silver lamé strapless dresses with slinky spike heels or leather miniskirts and thigh-high boots. I am wearing a red turtleneck sweater and blue slacks. My best outfit.

The fast dances are a wild frenzy. Every time a slow dance comes on, one man in particular asks a different woman to dance, leaving me for last. Everyone else is either sitting this one out or refilling their champagne glasses by that time. He tells me he saved me for last on purpose.

I know Garry and I are going to leave soon as our babysitter has a curfew even on New Year's Eve. But I feel something like excitement when this man holds my hand and leads me across the dance floor. "Killing Me Softly" by Roberta Flack plays on the stereo.

Strumming my pain with his fingers
Singing my life with his words

His name is Patrick. He is a policeman with a strong, muscular body, fitting for the job. He asks me if I know what the lyrics to the song mean. I think I do. It's about knowing what's in someone's mind without knowing them. It's about knowing where they hurt. He tells me I'm beautiful. This is the first time any person has told me I'm beautiful. I like the way it sounds when he says it. When we get home later that evening, I ask Garry to describe me.

"If you only had one word to describe me, Garry, what would it be?"

He's placing his keys on the tray of his wooden clothing valet and looks up at me, staring blankly.

"Just one adjective," I explain as he shrugs my question away. "How would you say I look?" I prompt, trying to help him along. Garry remains silent. "If you had to tell someone who hadn't met me what I looked like, what would you say?"

He finally answers but I am sorry I asked. "Plain. I'd tell them you are plain."

"Plain?" I say incredulously, raising my voice an octave.

Before I can form my next thought, Garry interjects, "And used baggage." This is the end of the conversation as he turns away from me and turns the TV on.

Patrick calls me the next Monday and says how much he enjoyed my company. He then suggests we get together. I want to be with him very much. I want to see myself through his eyes. But thinking about sex with someone who is not my husband, who is also married, which I judge to be wrong, has me even more worried about being like my father.

112   BABS WALTERS

Some of the men from the party, who have sons, are going on a father/son camping weekend. Patrick arranges for Garry and Adam to be invited. He tells me that most of the men think Garry is not man enough to fit in with them but love his large collection of VHS pornography and the portable VCR he freely lends out.

I arrange for Lindsay to stay with my friend Brenda, who has daughters her age, and Patrick meets me at the house.

I make dinner for him and immediately the conversation turns to the failures of our marriages, the attraction we have for each other, and what will happen next as I refuse to bring another man into my marital bed. Looking at us sitting at the dining room table eating beef stroganoff and chatting, we look like any married couple. That is, until the kiss. We are both breathless.

"I will find a neutral place for us to meet next time," Patrick promises, confident there will be a next time.

When I go to pick up Lindsay the next morning, my friend invites me to hang out at their pool. "Garry's not home and the girls are enjoying the pool."

I agree, and she lends me one of her bikinis. It almost feels like a day off, and I trust Brenda enough to tell her what's going on in my head.

We spend the day in the sun drinking pina coladas made by Brenda's husband, William. Then a barbecue for dinner. The day is long and the girls fall asleep from all the sun and fun. Brenda rolls a couple of joints and that frees me up to talk about Patrick.

She and William encourage me to experience having a lover. They share their private stories with me, of having sex with other couples. They don't think it's a big deal. *Everyone's doing it.* One minute I think yes. The next minute I think not. I am exhausted and my skin is burning from the sun. I say goodnight and head for the guest room. I'll spend the night and leave when Lindsay gets up in the morning.

It's not long afterward that Brenda comes in with a tube of aloe cream to soothe my sunburn. She begins to rub some on my back. It feels so good and cooling. I let her massage my legs and feet, too. When I turn over, her mouth is on mine. Her lips are soft and smooth, gentle and probing. She takes off her robe and lies next to me naked. Her breasts are beautiful. I am lost in her womanhood. We are tenderly exploring each other in the dark when the door opens and William comes in. This intrusion startles me. I sit up, pulling the sheet to my neck.

"No problem," he says. "I just want to watch."

"I think I should leave," I say, lost in the thoughts swirling around in my head like the circling eddies I see on the beach shoreline after high tide.

I gather Lindsay who's fast asleep and drive home thinking about Patrick, Brenda, my father. I wonder why it feels so good and different being with Brenda. Should I get involved with Patrick just because he makes me feel good about myself? Did the experience with my father interrupt my normal sexual exploration? Might I prefer women? Did I move too quickly with Garry just to get out of that house?

My life starts to spiral even more. I begin starving myself since it's the single place in my life where I feel like I have any control. Existing on only cigarettes and pot, I am a mess. I am beginning to think more and more that my children will be better off without me. My mind is filled with negative thoughts. I can't stop thinking about the same things obsessively. I repeatedly imagine I have inherited my father's disease. Or that I am negligent, like my mother. That I am crazy and probably hurting my children with all these sick thoughts and behaviors. Thoughts like these are in my head every waking hour, even keeping me from sleep again, becoming more intrusive into my daily functioning, so much so that I believe I can barely take care of myself let alone my children.

Chapter 14

My sister arranges for us to have a sit-down with my father to confront him for so-called satisfaction. At best, it will be closure.

She invites her new partner to come along for support. I worry that my father will bring one of his guns and kill all of us. So I ask Garry to come too. He refuses. I beg him. Anything he wants, I promise.

"You won't be here when I need you," he says, meaning to provide my wifely duties. "I'll have to take care of myself." Then, as if to clarify for my sake or to hurt me more, he says, "I'll have to masturbate."

With dread and an overwhelming sense of guilt, I agree to go to the meeting by myself.

I am sick to my stomach and have not been able to eat or sleep or even take care of my children adequately for days in anticipation of being shot by my father. I write love letters to my kids as my only way to describe what has happened and is happening to their mother. I mentally practice ending my own life. The only method that does not frighten me is the gas oven. I do not want my children to inherit the disease that runs in my family. I imagine they will be much better off without me.

Dear Adam and Lindsay,

Never forget, you are the two people I love the most, more than my own life. It has been my privilege to watch you pass through me into this world and grow into the people you are so far. Someday when you are parents, you will understand the miracle that children are. And the blessing it is to be an observer in their lives.

Parenting you has given me a second chance to be part of a loving family. Something I always wanted and dreamed about. You both have given me that gift.

One day, when you're older, you'll have questions about why I've left you the way I did. Just know that I left to spare you what I believed to be a genetic disease. One of mental illness. I want you both to grow up healthy: physically, mentally, and spiritually. I want you to have a chance to be part of another healthier, happier, loving family-to-be.

I don't know how to live with the pain I feel and have nothing more of myself to give you right now. So I give you the freedom to be loved and love again.

Your first mother,

Barbara

I drive around the block where my sister lives three times looking for a parking spot. It's not only my nerves that have me circling, unable to stop. It's also the fact that I am spatially impaired and need a lot of room to parallel park. My sister lives on a narrow street with retail stores filling the ground level and multiunit apartments above them. Every spot is taken, and several cars are even double-parked. Whoever planned this town did not anticipate the density of traffic these days. I finally find a spot five blocks away, and I'm a bundle of nerves, barely able to park my car.

The apartment is a walk-up. I take each step one at a time, resting and exhaling on each riser. When I reach my destination, I can barely lift my arm to knock on the door. *Maybe no one is home*, I pray. Of course, my sister opens the door.

"We've been waiting for you. Dad's already here."

I follow her, feeling like a condemned woman walking into her execution.

My first question is about a gun.

"I did not see one," Rhonda responds. "Let me lead the conversation," she continues, taking me into the room where my father waits. The light in the room is dim, giving the moment an ominous undercurrent. The only furniture is one small table, which doubles as an eating area and a workspace at other times. The three chairs fit very closely together with one side of the table against the wall. The middle seat is vacant and left for me.

I'd rather be anywhere but here, but I feel it is important to support my sister—and maybe I'll get some answers too. My heart is beating rapidly as I imagine all kinds of endings. A concealed gun, locked and loaded. A knife shoved deeply through my already weakened body. A brutal beating. As a less painful way of dying, for a moment I imagine the smell of gas when the pilot light is out, drawing me away from this room, hypnotic, making my head feel detached from my body.

While I'm running around in my own thoughts, I realize Rhonda and my father have begun talking and I'm missing what they are saying.

". . . why?" is all I catch.

"You don't know what my childhood was like," he says by way of explaining.

How could it be worse than ours? This meeting is a mistake. I can see he is just going to make excuses and blame others. He'll paint himself the victim. Isn't he sorry for what he did to us?

"It's because of your mother's frigidity. You don't know what it's like to be married to the cold bitch." With that, his anger starts to bubble up and pour out. His body presses forward and his face turns red. "Wait a minute," he changes direction, pounding his fist on the table and standing up. "I paid for the roof over your heads. I own you two. You are my chattel. Just like my goats or cows."

I can't believe what I'm hearing. He compares us to animals? I see daylight fading through the one uncovered window in the room. My father leans on the right side of the small table while Rhonda and I sit together toward the left. His normally large stature seems bigger somehow with him leaning over us in the small chairs. His upper body presses downward toward us, his shoulders hunch over as though he is prepared to lunge forward at any moment. He starts to speak again without making eye contact, talking to the empty space before him.

"You don't know what it was like to grow up with Manny and Anna." He pauses for effect, turns, and glares at us before looking away and continuing. "Manny was a hoodlum, raised on the streets. His foster family threw him out at age fifteen, when his own father stopped sending support money to them for him. He had no place else to go, so he found a stable to live in. With no human contact, he learned a lot about the horses. So much that he lied about his age then enlisted in the army, working in the cavalry division, caring for the horses that guarded our borders."

Always the storyteller, now with a captive audience, my father unwinds his tale. Rhonda and I listen. We have no other choice. But I imagine that she, like me, wonders what all this has to do with us and our childhood, and especially our father's behavior toward us.

"He was a rough-and-tumble kind of guy who had nowhere to go after the war. But he was known to face fights head on and got mixed up with some bad people." My father emphasizes the word *bad*, then looks at us to make sure we get the implications of it. "He saved his money to buy a truck and began delivering bootleg whiskey across state lines. That's where he learned to fend off hijackers and mafia goons with his fists and a gun."

Again my father looks at us and I know I'm right to feel threatened. "He and my mother were opposites. He handled everything with beatings. She became nervous and would cope by taking the dog out for a walk. That's why he took me to work with him regularly." My father sits down now and shows us the palms of his big hands as though they are worthy of display.

With a smile and look of pride, my father then tells us how he would play with the parts in bins in the hardware store that my grandfather managed, building machines out of the nuts and bolts, making new combinations and connections. This angered Manny who, according to my father, struck him "around the head." Manny reportedly took my father on deliveries with him, continuing the pummeling to quiet him, then left him to watch the truck while it was parked, illegally of course.

My father, always a very boastful and talkative person, continues with his elaborate tale of woe. "After my mother had a miscarriage, she became depressed. So my grandmother came to stay with us and take care of my mother and me. One day while she was singeing the feathers off a chicken, my grandmother caught on fire. I was five years old and stood there watching my grandmother burn to death, unable to do anything to help her." Rhonda and I have never heard this story before, but it is not what we came to this meeting to hear.

He continues, "Manny couldn't cope with my mother's moods and would need to escape. On these occasions, he would grab me and go on deliveries for hours. Except for one day, when he sent me up to make the delivery. I was eleven or twelve at the time, and the female customer opened the door and led me into her bedroom where she undressed me and forced me onto her bed. I was both aroused and frightened. But my erection betrayed me. And that was not the only time I was raped."

While my father grins, I feel sick again. I can't understand how any of this is being used as a rationalization for his behavior toward us. He hurt us as he had been hurt, but his smile confuses me. I feel my stomach bunching up like it is going to come up my throat.

"After my parents' divorce, I got in trouble in school when I built a pipe bomb from items I took from chemistry lab and shop." Again he looked at us, but this time beaming with pride apparently at how clever he was. "I stopped going to school because I was smarter than every teacher. They had nothing to teach me that I didn't already know. So my mother had me sent away to a reform school. That's where I met your mother. But it's also where I was attacked sexually by the school psychologist. At the reform school, they thought I had anger issues because of the bomb and sent me to this psychologist for help. He invited me into the gym's boxing ring and started jabbing at my midsection and punching my head like I told him Manny had. Well, I could only stand it for so long. I gave it right back to him. He couldn't admit defeat so he pushed me face down onto the mat, ripped my pants off, and, holding me down, raped me."

The room is getting darker and my mood even more bleak. It is eerie, and I feel like I did as a kid when we made up ghost stories to frighten each other.

For a split second, I feel sorry for the child my father had been. Then I'm boiling under the surface, angry that his legacy of hurt had to become our legacy, too.

"These were my lessons," he explains. "What I learned about how to behave from the adults in my life. I only did to you two what I was taught. How I was treated."

It's not lost on me that I know right from wrong while he doesn't. That I would never hurt my own kids, and he did.

Never one to run short on words, my father goes on, "Then there was your mother. I fell in love with her when we met at reform school, and when she became pregnant, my father gave me money to have her get an abortion. But we ran away to Maryland where we could get married instead."

My sister finally jumps in. "What kind of coed reform school lets teenagers sleep with each other?" I can think of so many questions I want to ask but this isn't one of them.

"Why was Mom sent to the reform school?" I interrupt, only to realize he's smiling. We've taken the bait. We're asking clarifying questions. We're not pressing him about the abuse. He's decidedly winning. He sits up straighter and speaks louder.

"Somebody found her making out under the stairwell in her apartment building and Grandma Nagler didn't know how to deal with that behavior." Then he shifts back to his story, returning to his agenda. "When I came back from Panama after the war, after sending her money, and her refusing to let me in the apartment, your mother emasculated me. She wouldn't let me in to see you. She had another man in there with her. I waited downstairs until he left. I think she was even sleeping with another boy in reform school. And then the cold, frigid bitch wouldn't perform her wifely duties anymore."

My father sits there blaming everyone but himself for all the abuse and suffering he inflicted. Still afraid he would harm us, I sit silent, choking on the words I want to say but I'm too scared to.

"How can you blame Mom for your perversion?" my sister demands. "For your sickness?"

With those words, he looks down at his hands, twisting them, one over the other, then starts to sob uncontrollably. His body is shaking so visibly that the table we're sitting at vibrates. We are sitting so close together that when his body leans to the left, he is touching me. I scooch toward my sister, not wanting to feel his body anywhere near mine. Why is he crying? It feels manipulative, and I think back to all the times he made us cry.

"What?" he asks. "What," he cries in between wracking sobs, "what are you going to do to me?"

He looks so pathetic wiping his eyes, nose, and mouth on his sleeve.

"What are we going to do to you?" I finally build up the courage to blurt out.

"Are you, are you going to turn me in, in to the police?"

His response is too much for me. I am raging inside. "I thought you were going to kill us tonight," I manage. "And you want to know what we're going to do to you?"

"Kill you?" he says. "If anything, I'm going to kill myself. I would never hurt you."

"Everything you did hurt us," Rhonda says. "We were just children. Children who needed to be protected from predators. Why didn't you find a woman your own age?"

"I could never go to other women. They wouldn't love me and protect me like you two did."

This is so wrong. I haven't eaten or slept in days, worrying I was going to be killed. I wrote notes to my children saying goodbye just in case. All my old childhood terrors have been reawakened this week. What was it all for? Had I expected remorse? An apology? Could any apology erase what happened? What about all the trauma his abuse caused that is still reverberating in my life?

The only significant takeaway from this meeting is that I now have a better understanding of where my parents came from. Of my father's disease. But that doesn't make me feel any better. In fact, I feel worse. Maybe I did inherit his disease. Maybe my children really would be better off without me.

I am shaking the whole drive home. "Breathe," I tell myself, noticing I'm holding my breath. Even after exhaling, my chest still feels so tight like it's holding something back. As tight as the violin strings I did not want to play and wound around and around until they broke. All I want to do is close my eyes and sleep for a very long time. Maybe I could wake up tomorrow and this will have been a dream. No, a nightmare.

Garry is waiting up for me when I get home. I don't know where to begin the story, but I don't need to.

"I had to take care of myself three times waiting for you," is the welcome I receive.

My head is aching. I can barely think. Not speak. *Too bad for you, you sick bastard. Too bad for all you sick bastards.* Holding my body as though pieces of me might flake off if I exhale, I wrap my arms around my chest and walk up the stairs to bed, not caring at all what Garry thinks anymore, or what he has to do without me—now or in the future.

I wait for Garry to leave with the children. They are going to visit his parents for the afternoon. I feel oddly at peace as I unfold what I'll do next.

The stove has a removable door for easy cleaning. I release the hinges on both sides and it comes off easily. There is a space between the right side and the wall next to the stove. I slide the door out of the way. I look for the opening on the bottom of the grill that leads to the gas feed below and blow out the blue flame. Sitting down on the floor in front of the oven, I stretch my head and neck as far inside as I can and reach up with my right hand, finding the center knob to turn on the gas. Winding the control clockwise all the way, I begin to breathe in the oddly sweetish smell. My chest and head go rigid, wanting to stop inhaling. To prevent me from breathing in. With effort, I take a deep one. I feel sleepy and close my eyes. My face feels raw, exposed as though the pores in my skin are expanding. My chest is heavy and contracted with my lungs squeezing hard to continue working. The smell is all I think about. The smell. Wavy lines of vibrating conductivity surround my skin. Crawling over me. Sleep is my last thought.

To his credit, when Garry arrives home and sees me lying on the kitchen floor in front of the stove with the gas on, he reacts swiftly. He turns off the flow and wakes me up.

"I had to come back for the photos," he tells me, referring to a gift for his parents, photos of the kids. "You are sick. Get yourself some help." Then leaves as planned.

He is right of course. I call Cynthia an hour later and make an appointment for her first available time.

Chapter 15

Cynthia's office feels like her: small, compact, and safe. There's a separate entrance from the street that I use for privacy.

The location is interesting. It's across the street from the public library, which feels familiar, like visiting Grandma Nagler in the Bronx again. Cynthia actually looks somewhat like Grandma Nagler, too, because of the Coke bottle–thick lenses in her glasses and her short curly hair. The only unfortunate part of her place in Morton Village is that my parents live about five blocks away. I would normally be afraid of running into my father, but I calm myself by remembering that he's at work during my appointment time. I try to relax. But I do think about it. I won't be ashamed if he finds out I'm in therapy. He's the reason, after all.

Because of the panicked call after my oven attempt and the letter I wrote to my little self as part of the women's empowerment group, Cynthia already has an idea why I'm here. She starts by asking me about the suicide attempt.

"You know I'm here to help you, Barbara. And recovery from a suicide attempt is never simple." She pauses before adding, "How do you feel right now about the way things turned out?"

I know Cynthia is referring to my failed attempt. And I have several mixed-up thoughts. *How could I risk letting my children find me in that position? Did I really want to die? Am I sick like I think my father is?*

We talk for a while. She is caring and understanding of my confusion and shame. Then she asks a final question before moving on:

124

"Do you have any more thoughts about ending your life or hurting yourself?"

Cynthia still needs to do an intake at our first appointment, to get my history, and I watch the clock use up the rest of my hour without getting the answers I came for.

After we're done with the formalities, she cuts to the chase. "Did something specific happen to push you to want to take your life?"

I know the answer and respond immediately, "It isn't one thing. It's several things happening at the same time that overwhelm me and leave me wondering if I am sick."

"Sick how?"

"Mentally," I say aloud for the first time. My teeth clench together, as though the word itself is abrasive to their cutting edges.

"What leads you to that conclusion?"

"I've been afraid of my sexuality because of what my father did to me when I was growing up. And all of a sudden I'm involved in sex outside my marriage and beyond my usual preference." There. I've said it. "My thoughts keep circling around that maybe I'm the same as my father. Maybe there's something in my genes, like an inherited disease."

"I can see why you're worried about yourself based on your father's sexual behavior. It also sounds like some of these negative thoughts are getting control of your well-being."

Cynthia explains that she is a CBT therapist, cognitive behavioral therapy, which addresses how our thoughts, feelings, and actions are all connected. "Our thoughts affect our emotions and feelings. We can work together to flip the script in your head. That way you'll be in control of your thoughts instead of allowing your thoughts to control you." She checks in and smiles before asking, "How does that sound?"

I am thinking about what she said when Cynthia explains further, "This is talk therapy." She puts aside the legal pad she has been taking notes on. "We will explore how your patterns of thinking and self-talk need to change in order for you to be less anxious or depressed. I'll give you strategies to work on in between sessions so you can begin making changes. How's that for our goal?"

My disappointment at not accomplishing anything today apparently shows.

"I know the first hour goes too fast with me needing your history and getting to know you."

The thought of working on strategies between sessions excites me though. Like the safety and diversion that school provided me. I ask for something to keep me focused on moving forward.

Cynthia smiles kindly at me. "What are you most afraid of happening next? Maybe we can work on that."

I do not have to think for long. "My biggest fear is that my father will try to take advantage of another girl. Maybe my daughter, Lindsay. Especially after he told us he chose us knowing that we would protect him."

"What would you do if you found out he was harming Lindsay?" she asks.

I had not thought about that before, but the answer comes quickly: "I would kill him."

"How?"

"I'd . . . I'd take the biggest carving knife I could find and stab him through his chest until he died." I expel a breath deep from my own chest, letting go of my fury at the thought of him hurting my child. If I have to kill him to protect my daughter, I know I can.

"Then that's what we'll work on next time," Cynthia promises. "I'll take care of all the details. You just take extremely good care of yourself until then. And if you think about trying to kill or hurt yourself again, call me right away, day or night."

I appreciate her offer to call her anytime but am still shaking. "I could use a hug. Is it okay if we hug?" I ask in a little girl voice choked with tears.

"It's not usual, but I think it is called for today," Cynthia explains before we embrace.

At my next appointment, Cynthia has a surprise for me. Sitting on the opposite end of the sofa from where I sat last time is a stuffed body in a red plaid flannel shirt. It is headless. The shirt and pants are men's and crammed full of newspaper.

"Who is this?" I ask, lifting my chin toward the faceless torso.

"This is a strategy prop we will use later." Cynthia's blue-gray eyes are smiling through her magnified lenses. I am confused but not afraid. "How was your week since we met last?" she asks.

"It was better than the week before." I don't say anything about how Garry has been avoiding me. Things at home are actually easier without his expectations. The children seem to be no worse for what happened. I destroyed the letters I wrote to them. Life goes on with laundry, food shopping, carpools, and doctors' appointments.

"Let's talk about the meeting with your father," she says, diving right into this, which I appreciate.

I relay what my father told us as though I'm delivering an outline. About his grandmother burning in front of him, his parents fighting and their different personalities, the reform school where he and my mother got together. About his own beatings and two rapes. About my mother's frigidity.

"How did his explanation make you feel?"

I pause to think about her question. I know I was angry. Especially that he blamed everyone except himself. But I was also angry with myself for not seeing how weak he was. For spending my life being afraid of this pathetic human being. I was angry that he felt no remorse for how he hurt us and how his behavior continued to hurt us. I was angry that even he could not hear or acknowledge us. Then, too, I felt self-loathing for choosing a husband just to get away from him. And now, how that husband, who was once kind and generous, is too immature to help me but can still be cruel and hurt me.

In the time I pause to think about her question, Cynthia adds her own thought, "I would have thought you'd feel very angry."

"I'm angry for so many reasons," I erupt now that she's prompted me. "At myself. At him. At Garry. At everybody who never listened or refused to see what was happening to me."

"Do you know what happens to anger when it's suppressed?" She looks directly at me, checking in for a response. When I don't answer, she continues, "It turns to depression when you literally press it down. That is probably where your depression has come from . . . from being angry. And unlike your father, you turn it inward on yourself."

This is a lot to contemplate. But it feels right. "So what do I do about my anger?" I ask, already trusting that Cynthia has a solution.

"Meet your father," she says, pointing to the headless effigy to my right. "If you're up for it, I'd like you to tell your father why you're angry at him. Say all the things you were just thinking of. What you're afraid he might do to Lindsay or another little girl. And then let's see how he reacts. Do you think you can do that?"

It sounds like a lot. I am hesitant. This is something I would never think to do on my own. But I am riled up and my skin is starting to crawl in search of relief.

"Let's start at the beginning. When was the first time your father hurt you?"

"Well, he believed my mother's complaints about me and hit me."

"Did he use his hands or something else?"

"It started with his hands but progressed to his belt."

"Using a belt must have hurt even more."

"It did. He would hit the back of my legs. Then he started pulling down my underwear at the same time. It was humiliating as well as painful."

Cynthia asks me one probing question after another, and I recount all kinds of injustices my father inflicted on me. Until we get to the reason for the prop she's brought in today.

"You were unable to confront your father's behavior before because you thought he would kill you as he threatened to do. You did what you needed to do to survive. But now you know he is weak and pathetic. How might you react if he molested Lindsay?"

I feel my body heat up with that thought. Like there is a fire blazing inside me. If I open my mouth, I think flames will shoot out like a dragon ready to charge.

"Picture what you would do if you found out your father even tried to touch Lindsay in an inappropriate way. Picture how you would feel not being able to protect your child against him. Picture all the times you were unable to stop him."

I am on my feet, not able to sit still. I need to move. I need action. That's when Cynthia pulls out a huge carving knife from a folder on the side of her chair and hands it to me. I know exactly what to do with it. I lunge at my father's stand-in and begin stabbing, slashing, screaming, "I hate you! I hate you!"

I'd always believed I was a bad girl, and that was the reason for my father's treatment of me. Now I realize it's because I am a good girl. He trusted me to cooperate and cover for him. That makes me even angrier now as I throw myself into this body. "How could you?" I begin to see his face on the torso. I knock him to the ground and slash away, making streamers and confetti out of his stand-in. I stomp and pull apart his insides until I am exhausted and almost collapse. Cynthia joins me on the floor and we both punch and pummel this lifeless being till only pieces are left and we are both sobbing softly.

After we're both breathing normally again, she breaks the silence. "How do you feel now?"

"Peaceful," I say. Then as an afterthought, I add, "I think I can really do it now if I have to. Thank you."

This is how my therapy begins, and my healing continues.

* * *

I feel emotionally and physically lighter now that the burden of helplessness has been lifted. No longer compelled to be the good child or the good daughter, I want to devote my energy to being the good wife. Maybe I can work things out with Garry. If I am a better wife, I can make him happier. I start exploring ideas. *What can I do to improve his life?* I wonder. What does he hate doing that I can take over for him? What would he like more of that I can ramp up on? Oh, it strikes me like the proverbial lightning bolt. I have two new moves in my plan.

Garry hates sending out invoices for his father's retail auto parts store. His illegible handwriting and tendency toward procrastination are contributing factors to late and unpaid bills. I talk to him about taking over the responsibility. First of all, I can do it during the day when Lindsay is in nursery and Adam in school. Second, I am not only good at math but also have great penmanship. He gladly agrees. I will find out whether my efforts are paying off in the following months when the customers' balances are lower. And while my goal originally stems from a desire to improve our relationship, I feel like I deserve some credit when we start seeing positive results. I ask Garry to pay me.

"I don't get to make that decision," he says, then adds, "It's my parents' business. Not mine."

I don't know where I get the cheek to push ahead, but I ask for something else. "I noticed officer certificates in the metal box with the checkbook and invoices. The least your parents can do with the way I'm helping the business is to make me treasurer or secretary if they can't pay me. I am bringing in money too."

They ultimately agree. A small victory. "It's just a piece of paper," I hear them say. It is more than that to me. It's a Corporate Officer Certificate. My role is formal in the company. And while I feel disappointed that it's not money, I let it go and move on to part two of my plan.

According to Maribel Morgan in her book, *The Total Woman*, published in1973, a wife becomes beautiful to her husband when she surrenders to him. I want Garry to see me as beautiful, so I don't need to look outside our marriage for that validation. I try the hardest trick from the book. I buy the largest box of Saran Wrap I can find. Do my hair and makeup in party mode. Then, standing in front of the full-length mirror, starting from above my knees, I unroll the clear plastic wrap from front to back and round and round until my entire naked body is covered. I struggle to step into my high heels, having made the wrap a little too tight, but greet him at the door just as he arrives. Garry just shrugs and walks past me. He has brought four new plastic airplane and tank models with him, his latest hobby.

"I'll be in the basement spray painting them. Can't wait to show them to Adam in the morning." He heads downstairs, preferring camouflage and decals for these toys to being real with me.

Both my ploys to get him to love and acknowledge me have fallen flat.

I still feel bolder now that I think my father is out of the way, both from the confrontation and the mutilation. So I decide it's time to approach my mother. I call and invite her to lunch. She sounds pleased.

"Oh. How nice. Can you pick me up, sweetheart?"

I would much prefer to meet her at the restaurant so if things get tense, I can leave. But knowing I am going to bring up topics she will not want to face, I acquiesce, hoping to relax her enough to speak the truth.

When I pick her up, it's clear my mother has taken great care in her dress: a pair of white capri pants with a silky floral print top and a large white wide-brimmed straw hat. She tells me the outfit is new for the occasion. Her announcement feels weird given my agenda. Clearly, she expects a lovely mother-daughter afternoon out.

At the restaurant, we find a table apart from the others in the back corner. "This way we can hear each other talk," I explain to her.

After checking the menu and ordering, I wade into the conversation I want to have.

"I realize I don't know much about your childhood and hoped you could share a little about it with me."

"What do you want to hear about?" she asks cautiously, stretching the timing between words.

"Well, what was it like to be little Lilly? School, friends, family?"

She thinks for a moment, turning her head to the side and tilting her chin up, lifting the corner of the hat brim. "Well, you know, I was very athletic. I loved basketball and roller skating and preferred playing with my brother and his friends to girls."

This is the most I have ever heard my mother say at one time. Surprised, I smile and encourage her to go on. "Basketball. That's a little unusual for girls of your generation. Isn't it?"

"To me it was all about staying out as late as I could, away from the apartment. We could play in the schoolyard until it got dark and then run home."

"I remember the apartment as being a small living space for five people. Is that why you wanted to stay away?"

"No," my mother answers quickly. And then tells me why.

Chapter 16

My mother's words are rationed out as though she doesn't know where to find the answer, as though it lies very deep somewhere hard to reach. As though she doesn't know when the next word will come along. It is a painful process to watch. If I did not already know her, I would say she's mentally slow. I suddenly realize where the expression "pulling teeth" comes from as I can feel mine start to clench and my jaw tighten.

"So why did you want to stay away from home?" I prompt.

Another pause as I watch her eyes look around, searching for how to start, how to explain.

"My parents fought a lot." It's as if there's a limit to how many words can come out at the same time.

"That doesn't seem all that unusual." I try to move it along. "They did get divorced." My mother doesn't answer so I push. "Did they fight in front of you?" What was so terrible? I wonder what she's afraid to say.

"Yes," she finally says. "My father didn't like her teaching me how to help in the kitchen. He thought that was beneath his children."

I see there's more to the story and remain quiet, giving her space, as uncomfortable as it makes me. I watch our waitress seating other diners, wondering if their presence is inhibiting my mother.

Despite my distraction, she continues, "One time," she hesitates again, "my mother was teaching me how to peel potatoes, and he took the peeler out of my hand. Then threw it at her. She started to whine, saying she was sorry. As gentle as he was with me, he got rough with her."

"Rough in what way?"

"He . . . he . . . did something terrible. He opened the kitchen window, pushed her against the windowsill, and . . ."

Even I take a deep breath picturing the scene. My gentle grandmother near the open window. I want to cry.

"He pushed her backward over the windowsill," she says again. "And then . . . and then he leaned her body out the window, threatening her. If she ever treats me like the help again, he said, he would throw her out."

When my mother pauses, my stomach is bunched in knots so tight, I feel my body drawing in, protecting itself.

"That's when I started to shake." There is more to the story. "It started with my hands, then my whole body started to shake so hard I couldn't stand. It traveled up my arms. My head and legs were vibrating. From small tremors, the feeling grew into what they later called seizures."

I don't want to feel sorry for her. I don't want to believe her. I want her to hear me. Be my witness. Mother me. That's why I called this meeting. She has reversed the agenda.

In frustration, I pick at my salad even though it no longer looks appealing. I am moving the lettuce around the plate when she drops the bomb.

"They had to take me to the hospital right away. Right after he threatened Grandma and I started to shake. The doctor said I had Saint Vitus's dance." My mother swallows hard before adding, "It's a nervous disorder."

I've never heard of this before, and wonder if it's even legitimate, but try to show compassion in spite of my hesitation. "What did they do for Saint Vitus's dance?"

"There was no cure. Only treatment. Two weeks of bedrest and avoidance of traumatic experiences."

Well, that explains the woman sitting across from me, my mother.

"That sounds like a terrible experience, Mom. But what about the horrible experiences Rhonda and I had growing up?"

She responds so quickly it sounds defensive. "Like what?"

"Like the lack of supervision, the beatings, the escape to Florida, the night visits from Dad." I purposely leave out her neglect, sacrificing us to protect herself. I leave out how she encouraged him to hit us, how she ran away with a lover, how she made us lie about that lover being our new father. How she moved us five times before I was seven. How we had no food, no home, no attention to our needs.

"He beat me, too," is all she says. I notice she starts to twist her hands together. She is stopping them from shaking, pressing them down onto the surface of the table. One over the other. Saint Vitus's dance again?

"He may have hit you, but you told him to hit us. You invited him."

"I had no choice." But then, as if it were a Hail Mary, she says, "I did get a court order to protect us."

"What about all the times you went out with your lover? And left us with Mrs. Cruz. She didn't feed us or supervise us. She didn't protect us from the neighborhood kids taunting us about how many funny uncles we had that visited you when we were in school."

"I didn't know about any of that."

"Well, you knew about Larry and running away to Florida. Telling us to lie about his being our father. Watching him beat Rhonda."

"I took you with me. I could've left you behind. If I had, Larry would've stayed with me." This is said all in one breath, and she exhales forcibly.

"Did you take care of us when you didn't protect us against Dad having sex with us?" I am relentless and won't let her off the hook now.

"I didn't know about any of that either. I am naïve sexually. I couldn't have even imagined something like that."

The waitress arrives to see if we are finished with our food. I answer for both of us. There is no room in my knotted stomach for anything else to go down. Once she leaves, I confront my mother with facts.

"I know that you read my diary. How can you say you didn't know? How can you say you were sexually naïve? You got pregnant at seventeen. Had extramarital affairs."

"I never read your diary." She says this looking down where her lunch sat momentarily ago and shaking her head.

"Then how did you know when I cut school? How did you know I was smoking? Or if I met boys when you were away?"

She pauses, takes a sip of her iced tea again, summoning her response. "Those are things teenagers do. I was a teenager once, too. I just remembered and guessed."

We are both frustrated and spent, like we've gone ten rounds in the ring. It doesn't feel like I will get any satisfaction today.

"What do you want me to do?" she pleads. "Do you want me to leave him?"

The only expectation I have for this meeting is to hear her side, her reason, for the way she behaved or failed to act. I want to hear her say she is sorry for not protecting us better. Her questions demonstrate to me how much I have to be the one responsible for solving her problems. I am back in the closet the first day of kindergarten, realizing I cannot count on my mother.

As an afterthought, she explains, "I can't leave him. I have no skills, no money. And I can't be alone. Can't be without a man."

She is sobbing softly and shaking now, so I choose my answer carefully. "I don't know how you can stay with him, knowing that he had sex with your two daughters."

"Well," she says, a small smile forming at the corner of her lips. "At least he's not hurting you anymore. You got away. It's over for *you*."

The emphasis on the word "you" lands like a punch to my chest.

FACING THE JAGUAR

*   *   *

When I get home, I am still spinning. Both my parents want me to feel sorry for them. But they have no compassion for me.

I invest myself in making a great dinner for my family. I could use some comfort, too.

When Garry arrives home from work, he's carrying plastic bags filled with saltwater fish. His new pets. They are beautiful. Royal blue. Bright yellow. Red sea anemones. He has spent hundreds of dollars experimenting on getting just the right pH balance for these exotic creatures to live in. So far, they all die. They are extremely delicate.

"You're late," I say, explaining why the kids have already eaten and the food is somewhat dry.

"I had a tough day," is all he says.

"So did I." But I don't say anything more.

"But I bring in the money that keeps a roof over our heads."

Recognizing that I've heard this message before, and already angry, I can't help myself. "And that lets you spend hundreds on fish that always die?"

"I worked for the money, and how I spend it. You know how I get this extra money anyway. I have to spend it quickly under the table, on things with no record or receipt."

I have a new recurring dream. It is evening and there is a knock at the front door. Two police officers in their dark blue uniforms are standing on the top step leading into the house. I assume they are collecting for the Police Benevolent Association.

"Are you Mrs. Walters?" the one closest to me asks.

I am surprised he knows my name and I stand there frozen for a moment, trying to figure out how that's possible. There is no name on the door or mailbox.

"Can we come in?" he asks, and they both take a step forward.

This is highly unusual for soliciting donations, but they are authority figures. So I allow them inside. They remove their hats and the one who has been speaking asks if we can go sit down in the living room.

My heart starts to accelerate the way it does when I haven't had a chance to be fully prepared for every eventuality. The two officers sit across from me while I listen to the grandfather clock tick the seconds away. This is beginning to feel ominous. Silence and ticking. Heartbeats and ringing ears. Have I seen this scene in an Alfred Hitchcock movie?

The officer that spoke before clears his throat. "We're sorry to be the bearer of bad news. But there's been a robbery and shooting at your husband's place of business." He waits to make sure I am following. "Mr. Walters has been shot. He was taken by ambulance to Brunswick Hospital. But unfortunately," he stops again, perhaps for his sake, as well as mine, "Mr. Walters was dead on arrival."

I let in what I just heard and surprise myself with only one question. "When you say Mr. Walters, you're talking about my husband, Garry, and not his father, Peter?"

"It is definitely the junior. But we will need you to accompany us to identify the body."

"I will need someone to watch my children," I explain, taking some time to regulate my emotions. I move and speak like a zombie, expressionless except for eyes wide open focused inward in deep thought.

I go into my bedroom and close the door to use the turquoise princess phone on my nightstand. How can I call anyone and tell them what just happened without them hearing what's going on inside me?

I am finally free. From Garry and my marriage. From all the problems inherent in potentially leaving him. I no longer have to worry about his parents trying to take my children from me . . . something I have been worried about ever since they found out my family history. I also have a stock certificate now saying I am an officer of the business. With Garry gone, I can start my own life over and get it right this time.

At my next visit with Cynthia, we discuss my dream.

"Am I a horrible person?"

Of course, she says no. "It's just a dream. You did not actually kill anyone."

"But I was happy he was out of my way without me having to do any of the work."

"If you really want to be free from your marriage, you will have to do the work. The dream is a message, an indication of something you want. Let's not panic, but also let me know if you have the dream again."

"I have had it several times," I admit, "and each time it gets more and more vivid."

"We can work on your true feelings and desires about your marriage. But there is one thing I want you to know and consider. The planet is big enough for both you and Garry to exist apart without one of you having to die."

I like the sound of that and fall into trying to figure out what I need to do next since Garry is not dead and my dream is not a reality.

"How did that meeting with your mother go last week?"

I love that Cynthia remembers everything I say. "We never could agree on anything. So I don't know why I thought this time would be any different."

"Mother-daughter relationships are notoriously difficult."

That may be true, but it doesn't make me feel better about mine.

"What fairy tale do you remember from childhood that feels the most like you and your mother?"

I think of Snow White, then Hansel and Gretel, but finally say aloud, "Cinderella!"

"Why Cinderella?"

"I often felt like Lilly was my wicked stepmother expecting me to do all the work while she went to parties and had fun."

"Here's something interesting for you to consider. In every one of those fairy tales we grew up with, the mother is always mean and self-serving. But the daughter is always beautiful and wins out. It's easy to understand how the mothers are resentful of their daughters' youth and potential. Especially since your mother became pregnant as a teenager."

"Do you think my mother is jealous of me?"

"I do. Specifically because her life happened to her and she feels she has no options left while you have all of yours ahead of you." Cynthia always makes good connections. "Can you give me an example from childhood where your mother involved you in something she was interested in but you were not?"

It's not hard to reach for a story. "When I started high school, I wanted to study French. All the French students were also part of the chorus. But my mother wanted me to study Spanish, which meant I had to learn an instrument. The kids taking Spanish were part of the orchestra or band. I needed something small that I could carry back and forth, inexpensive to rent, and she picked the violin. I hated it."

As I remember more, I continue, "She sent me for lessons, but I was terrible at it. To encourage me to stick with it, she bought the two of us tickets to a violin concerto. I hated that too. When I looked to my left and saw her sitting next to me, she was beaming like she was in seventh heaven."

Cynthia weighs in. "I'd like to propose that you wanted something more at this meeting from your mother. You wanted her approval or acknowledgment that you are good. That's what has been driving you to always be more and do better. That's where your feelings of never enough come from. Even if you've never said it out loud. It's been your driving philosophy."

"What do you mean?"

She looks directly at me, smiling as she continues, "You are like the little girl walking down the street with two handfuls of colorful marbles. There in front of her on the sidewalk is the most beautiful of all marbles. She tries to decide which one of the marbles in her hands she is willing to give up. She looks back and forth between them, unable to make up her mind. Then she gets an idea. Lifting up the hem of her dress, she drops each handful into it. Then she uses her free hand to pick up the extra one. No matter what you have or do, it always feels like its never enough to you. I think you wanted your mother to tell you how good you are. And, you wanted her to be a good mother who wouldn't let something bad happen to her children."

I sit quietly, letting the possibility that Cynthia is right sink in. "I just want my mother to be motherly." It sounds pathetic.

"Just because a woman's body is capable of having a baby doesn't mean she is emotionally ready to. And not every woman has a maternal instinct. From what you tell me, your mother not only did not have that instinct but also neglected you. Probably one of the reasons you chose a partner who is also emotionally negligent." Taking a different tack, she asks, "What attracted you to Garry in the first place?"

"I saw him as a way out of my home and family. As kind and generous."

"And maybe a little naïve or easy?" Cynthia gets right to the point.

"Yes. That, too, looking back. I don't think I thought about that at the time."

"What were the good parts about being married to Garry besides getting out of your house?"

"Well, I did get out. Not far enough away, though. Without question, Adam and Lindsay. The very best part of my life. The only decisions I would make over and over again."

"Because you had to fend for yourself, you may feel emotionally lonely. In spite of the simple ways Garry shows his love for you. That responsibility does not fall on him, though."

Here she goes again. Shooting piercing arrows right through me. I let what she says penetrate my desire to defend myself. And I wonder: *Where do I begin and end in my discordant marital equation? Will I ever be capable of feeling loved? Or am I being misled by my fantasy of love?*

Chapter 17

We take our shoes off and start walking west along the Great South Bay. The air is cool and the sun is warming. We are silent, enjoying the silky sand between our toes, the plovers scurrying all in a row on their tippytoes. They run in a line toward the water, then hurry back as every wave rushes in. My new friend Carolynn, the clinical social worker aka tennis-league hypnotist, asks me a question that seems to be pulled out of the blue from the vast bay being fed by the ocean beyond it.

"Did you believe your father's account of his childhood? The one he told your sister and you as an explanation for his behavior?"

Without having to think about it, I answer immediately, "Yes." His details were too amazing to be entirely made up. His stories, though, had always been bigger than life. He had a talent for holding his audience. It was the way he told stories . . . the way his big voice filled the room and engulfed the air around him. The way he magnified his importance no matter the circumstances. The way he held back critical information, imprisoning his audience with those tethers. So yes, I did believe his story. But then as we keep walking, her question sits with me like a holiday meal too quickly eaten, pressing against my diaphragm, pushing up into my ribs. That's when a bright light bulb flashes on, illuminating my reality. It's not uncommon to be held hostage by a skilled manipulator, especially when his target is as empathetic as I happen to be.

After the walk, I decide to see what I can find out about my family for myself. I've had some practice at successfully capturing and verifying portions of my parents' history without their cooperation or assistance.

The first resource I turn to is the gift of four volumes' worth of Grandmother Walters's diaries. They came my way because I'm the oldest grandchild and also because nobody else wanted them. The first two tiny blue and black book covers each boast the words: *Five-Year Diary.*

My grandmother wrote to the very bottom of each page, even squeezing some words into the final half line of the lowest margin. The second two books, the red and brown leatherette Deskaides, the diaries that I remember from childhood, have dried out bindings and are from the years my father was still living at home. Many of the pages are loose. But all are dated, even if she had to change the dates to match the length of her ideas for the day and the fullness of her schedule. On the inside of each mini volume are phone numbers and birthdates penned in ink for safe keeping.

Grandma mostly recounted her daily routine of cooking, cleaning, and visiting neighbors. Although there are many entries on the topic of my father's truancy, I find something of interest from December 1941, particularly December 8. About not being able to get my father up and to school in the morning, she wrote:

Happy when Mr. Altrowitz (the truant officer) took him to school in the afternoon. Jay also had to report to the Jewish Board of Guardians for an interview about acceptance to the special school.

It was a tough day, beyond the difficulty with my father. She added,

President Roosevelt spoke over the radio noontime announcing WAR on Japan after Japan declared WAR on America yesterday. Had to lie down in the afternoon. I'm so tired.

FACING THE JAGUAR

December 9, 1941: *"Couldn't get Jay to school again. Though children were sent home early from school on account of air raid drills and scare of fifty airplanes overhead. Didn't know if they were Japanese."*

December 15, 1941: *"Happy when Mr. Altrowitz took Jay to school. I can't manage him anymore."*

December 25, 1941: *"Jay was very cranky and nasty to me in the afternoon again. Made my Christmas Day miserable."*

I picture my tiny grandmother, how she looked the last time I saw her sitting at her secretary desk, telling me that someday I would have a diary of my own too. Not sharing hers at the time because it was "private." I wonder what she would think of me reading it now to validate my father's history.

Many more entries follow detailing my father not wanting to go to school. So that is on the record. His explanation to us that he thought he was smarter than all the teachers, I cannot verify.

The Jewish Board of Guardians who he had an appointment with did exist in the 1940s, addressing a broad spectrum of issues that affected teenagers, including truancy from school.

Apparently the reform school my parents threatened Rhonda and me with on a regular basis every time we deviated from their unrealistic expectations was a reform school after all. After reading my grandmother's journals, I ask my therapist Cynthia to look up the school in her books on psychiatric institutions. She helps me find a listing for the actual school. It was billed as a private school for troubled teens and juvenile delinquents.

Once I have the name of the school, I continue the research on my own. I discover that the girls' campus was founded in 1911 as a correctional facility, in response to what its founders saw as a rise in delinquency among young Jewish women.

Alarmed by reports of the growing numbers of young females arraigned in New York City's children's courts, the concerned advocates established a Jewish girls' correctional facility comparable to the already-existing boys' campus. This Jewish reformatory for boys had opened in May 1906 in Hawthorne, New York. I learn that the school, one of the first such institutions in the country, was built on the cottage or group living plan and was widely acclaimed for its emphasis on rehabilitation, rather than punishment, in the treatment of troubled youngsters.

Beyond truancy, teens were housed there for reports of disorderly conduct, peddling, improper guardianship, incorrigibility, immorality, stabbing, assault, and petty larceny. These youngsters, according to a longtime school president, were "not hardened criminals, but only children deprived of their natural heritage and rights." I never thought of my parents as being deprived in any way especially after I received so much from three of my grandparents. The benefactors involved in this work attributed rising Jewish juvenile delinquency to the difficulties experienced by recent immigrants as they adjusted to life in the United States.

Or more accurately, incompatibility between immigrant parents and their American-born children. It sounds like a generation gap between the old and the new. The aim of the school was to give every child the opportunity to readjust themselves and to return to the community as useful and self-respecting members.

A while back, I was given immigration documents for my grandparents for safe keeping. As the oldest child, I put them in a file folder and never looked at them again. I pull them out now to find these Ellis Island documents confirm that three of my four grandparents were immigrants transplanted from England, Czechoslovakia, and Hungary, though their children were all born in the States.

With the help of the reference librarian, I am guided to tomes on immigration from Eastern Europe after WWI. There I read that many people in that area were faced with economic and political unrest as well as lack of opportunities. That last fact pulled them toward the United States and its reputation as "the land of opportunity." My Grandfather Nagler's manifest sheet says he traveled on the TSS *Bremen* which was part of the Hamburg-American Line. I find an affidavit stating he had a job waiting for him as a butcher with Carl Weisbacker for $45.00 per week. The library books say their journey traveling by steamship across the Atlantic Ocean was often arduous and perilous. Then once they were processed through Ellis Island, they had to adjust to a new culture, a new way of life, and a new language.

To assist with their transition, I learn that Hungarian immigrants established social clubs in their tight-knit communities. My maternal grandparents met at an Austro-Hungarian community dance. I also learn that Czechoslovakian immigrants were known for their education and skilled trades. That was true for my grandfather who had graduated from gymnazium, our equivalent of a four-year university degree.

The public library is also a secondary resource when no other relatives are left to or care to answer my questions. I find my father's name listed in a class roster for two of the years he lived at the private school but not my mother's.

Like a detective, my curiosity spurs me on. Wherever possible, I question direct witnesses. For example, my oldest cousin, who is also my father's youngest cousin, was alive when their grandmother set herself on fire. The story that was communicated among the family was that my grandmother had just suffered a miscarriage. Her own mother, my father's grandmother, came to stay with the family to help out while her daughter healed. It was during the preparation of a chicken dinner that the fire began.

Because we live in different states, I phone my cousin to hear if her words match what my father said happened. In her measured Trentonian cadence, pausing after every few words, here is what she recounts:

"Barbara, remember this is what I heard but did not directly witness." I make a sound of understanding so she can continue. "In those days, chickens were bought whole with feathers still on them. You selected the one you wanted hanging from a hook at the poulter's and took it home to clean before cooking. Clean meant plucking the feathers off. The easiest way to do that was to use the flame on the gas stovetop to singe or burn the feathers off." My cousin stops here, making a nasal sound of displeasure to show how nasty burnt chicken feathers smell. "Like hair on fire. Nobody knows exactly how it happened but somehow Grandma's sleeves or apron caught fire and went up in large flames before help could arrive. Your father was five years old at most and just stood there frozen, watching the fire engulf Grandma."

My father seemed to feel the explanation of his behavior started at this point in his life. I know what it's like to be five and have a life-altering day in the kindergarten coat closet, so I believe this part of his account to be true.

There was no one else in the kitchen to explain my father's reaction. Was he terrified? Mesmerized? Too inexperienced to know what to do?

We do know that signs of early trauma in a child include trouble regulating emotions. Kids who have experienced trauma may also start to avoid school, not wanting to leave their family, possibly explaining his truancy habit. But I don't think anyone recognized how awful this experience must have been for my father. After all, they were dealing with a miscarriage and a death—much more immediate issues.

Would any of us have known what to do as a five-year-old to

stop a fire without injuring ourselves or making it worse? Was my great-grandmother screaming and making the situation even more alarming? Had my father just asked a question at the wrong time and distracted her? Did he feel like it was his fault? Did he cover up for those feelings of guilt all his life? Did he disassociate, cut off from his panicked feelings from that moment, causing him to become unfeeling of others' pain in the future? Can one dramatic, traumatic event in a child's early life, cause them to abuse other vulnerable children?

The conversation with my cousin sends me back to reread my grandmother's journals looking for more clues. It takes me days to go through all the years. She has one more entry that validates a different part of my father's description. That of his own father. I could hear her soft, gentrified voice saying, "Not in front of the kinder, dear," when discussing adult-rated themes. In this entry, her older sister is giving her advice about being alone after the divorce. "Stop crying. Forget about the bully husband, the brutish ruffian, and move on with your life. You're better off without him." That matches my father's description of the man who delivered his beatings.

And as crazy as it sounds, I remember hearing of fathers who arranged for introductions to sex for their sons at about the same age as my father said he was raped. I can certainly relate to having sex forced on you when you are not ready. I cannot confirm this is what happened. But find myself wondering about my father using this event as justification for his treatment of us and the type of fathering he received.

I think back over my own interactions with my paternal grandfather. Whenever I visited his home in New Jersey, he would spend all his time outside with the chickens and pigs he was raising, never paying attention to me. I remember hearing that in addition to the horses he cared for during the war, my grandfather opened a business raising mice and rats for medical lab tests. He built his own cages and got his sons to clean them. Because doctors only wanted pure white animals, if a latent gene produced a multicolored one, the boys were able to take them as pets.

My father explained what he and my uncle did with those animals: "We took them to school and scared the girls. Or when there were too many, we disposed of them."

I remember having a longer interaction with my grandfather when Garry and I were planning our wedding. We met first with the rabbi who a year later would not help me get my sister out of harm's way. Before the wedding though, Rabbi Spielman wanted us to prove that we were not related given that both our last names were the same. It wasn't funny at the time, but in hindsight it struck me that he was worried about us being cousins and too closely related by blood to marry. He wanted us to prove that our grandfathers were not brothers. And since my grandfather never knew his parents, they certainly could have been.

After our meeting with the rabbi, I asked my grandfather to see if he could find out who his parents were. He was able to do that much for me. His father was a British Merchant Seaman and his mother an Irish maiden. They clearly were not Jewish. Or married.

Garry found out that his family had their name changed when they landed at Ellis Island. They spoke with a heavy Eastern European accent and had their name changed from Volter to the more American-sounding Walters.

I was beginning to think my grandfather might be a good person until he refused to come to my wedding if I invited his ex, my grandma.

"I will not follow that woman down the aisle."

"Then you can go first, Grandpa," I offer.

"I will not have that woman staring me down behind my back."

"Would you rather not march down the aisle, Grandpa? You don't have to," I try.

"The only way I come to the wedding is if that woman is not invited."

I hesitate before reacting. "That's an impossible choice."

"Well, it's your choice."

He could not stand to be together in the same room with my grandmother and his new wife. When we refused to comply, we never saw him again. He was apparently a tyrant, the my-way-or-the-highway kind of guy that my father described.

After I dive into my father's past to corroborate what I can, I decide to look at what my mother told me and see what I can find. My mother's story of her illness had some veracity behind it. It turns out that Saint Vitus's dance is a real nervous condition that is now called Sydenham chorea. It's a childhood movement disorder as an inflammatory response to strep throat or rheumatic fever and is characterized by rapid, involuntary, irregular movements of all muscles. The reason most of us have never heard of it is that it is much less common today than it was in the past. When it does occur, the symptoms are typically less severe and the relapses less frequent than they would have been when she was first diagnosed.

Most of the articles I research say that untreated rheumatic fever or strep is the most common culprit. Of course, with antibiotics, there are fewer cases, except in developing countries where drugs and care are less available. Bed rest, sedatives, and medication to control the erratic movements are usually prescribed. This pretty much matches my mother's description of her seizures. Of course, not what brought them on in the first place.

It is generally considered to be characterized by an abrupt onset. It is easy to see how my mother associated it with her own mother being hung backward out the kitchen window. And to equate seizures with her father's threats to her mother. Their daughter was to be treated like royalty, doing no form of servant's work and provided the bed rest and no-stress regimen recommended by the doctors. Something my mother believed was her survival formula. As an adult, she expected me to give her comfort, the kind due a child . . . for me to be the parent and have no expectations of her. Both my parents were out of touch with how they made us feel.

For parents to accurately imagine what their children need and feel, they need to be aware of their own emotional development and shortcomings. My parents' tough defenses were probably built to cover up any vulnerability and loneliness from their own childhoods.

I call my mother's younger sister, curious to confirm the episode of Saint Vitus's Dance disease and subsequent hospitalization.

"I was five years younger than your mom. But I remember the shaking. It was horrible and very frightening. They took her to the hospital where she stayed for a couple of weeks, I think." She pauses as though she's thinking of something else, then she adds, "I also remember your mother going to a sleepaway school and then leaving to get married. Not returning home."

All this exploration into my parents' generational trauma triggers an old memory of making kreplach with Norma. The story she related comes back to me about how she was depressed and cried for prolonged periods of time when both her parents died during her pregnancy with Garry. I know that we do not have to live the experience of our parents or ancestors to have the trauma embedded somehow in our cellular memory. Could this explain Garry's distant, immature, and self-centered behavior when I needed his emotional support the most? He was so kind before my problematic family drama unfolded.

Two weeks later, I call Carolynn to go for a walk and catch her up on what I discovered. But something is bothering me, and I don't start with my fact finding.

"I always felt like my mother resented me. Like she preferred my sister and brother to me. She had a habit of telling me all the wonderful things my siblings did for her, their calls, their gifts. Then I found out she did the same thing to them. Pitted us one against the other."

FACING THE JAGUAR

I'm mulling over this insight when Carolynn stops and asks her usual kind of doozie question: "What do you think it was like for your mother being a teenager and unwed?"

I know that my parents ran away to Baltimore to get married without needing parental permission. I happened to arrive a month before they could accomplish that goal. Soon she was alone with me when my father got drafted into the army.

"Do you think she was afraid?"

Whose side are you on? I wonder, though I don't say this aloud. My first impulse is no. She resented me. I made her a prisoner of a life she did not want and a man she was sorry to have tied herself to. Then I wonder who rejected who first? I did find her lacking as a mother. I have report cards from early elementary school commenting on her poor parenting skills. Teachers complained that she had been warned multiple times about my cleanliness and health habits.

"I guess she might have felt in over her head, unprepared to be a parent at seventeen," I concede. Maybe she did not resent me. Maybe I judged her and held her to an impossible ideal.

Overall, neither of my parents apologized or accepted any responsibility for their behavior. They both protested that they were victims of the circumstances of their lives and held the position that they had tough lives too. With maturity, therapy, and self-development, I would learn to forgive them their limitations. They did the best they could. Unfortunately, their best wasn't very good.

But even more important, I would learn to forgive myself. For what, you ask? For the shame of hating my body, allowing it to be used to betray me. For not protecting myself or my sister. For subsequent decisions I made and the ones I failed to make. For some really dark, scary places I have found myself in.

* * *

Continuing the walk, Carolynn tells me a fable she knows—the grandfather game.

A man becomes a successful doctor and builds a mansion filled with beautiful possessions. When his father needs a place to live, the man makes room for his father. Whenever the man entertains, he notices how his father does not fit in with the educated friends who are invited.

The man moves his father into the basement of the house to make his immigrant beginnings less obvious or to hide him away. Eventually even this arrangement invites inspection. The man then moves his father to the stables with the horses.

One day the man comes home from work and finds his little son filling a shoe box with manure. "What are you doing?" asks the man of his son. "You have so many wonderful toys to play with."

"I'm playing the grandfather game," says the child innocently. "You put the grandfather in a box and shovel horse poop on top of him."

This is not a lesson I want to teach my children. I don't want them to treat me the way I treat my parents. I am left thinking about what my bitterness shows the kids. And I think I understand why Carolynn, always the teacher, wants me to be more forgiving of my parents.

Anger is a double-sided weapon. You may think you are aiming it at another person, but all that energy you are expending is harming you at the same time. My job is to continue to heal. To continue to give meaning and purpose to what happened to me. I am not what happened to me. I am resilient, unstoppable, unsinkable, and strong. Shining my light in some very dark places. And on the way, moving forward with compassion.

Epilogue

I remember standing on a milk crate to reach up and see out the small round peephole in the front door of our apartment in the Bronx when I was nine years old. The lens was only big enough for one eye to peer through. The other eye had to be closed at the same time. The convex glass magnified everything on the outside in the hallway, making whatever was out there look larger than life. This reflects well my point of view throughout my childhood: straining, thinking I could see the whole world if I concentrated. If I focused on looking out. Now in my seventh decade, I have the benefit of a wide-angle, panoramic lens. I can see the entire landscape before me from side to side and even turn back to capture the view behind me.

I didn't grow up thinking my childhood was terrible. I thought it was tougher than most and challenging, but thanks to the heroines in the stories I read, I believed I would triumph one day. Just as they did. Although some fairy tales frightened me with witches, beasts, and supernatural creatures, these stories also filled me with my greatest hopes and dreams. They transported me to another place, away from my home, so that I could escape my reality. "Once upon a time" drew me in and landed me in "happily ever after."

I believed that all heroines, in spite of their distress, endured their pain and learned their lessons. Instead of escaping their reality, their duty, my role models embraced their hard work and ultimately found rewards in the forms of princes aka husbands. On the flip side, these tales depicted many mean, cruel, and messed-up human beings, which made my family life feel somewhat more normal.

Folk tales and legends were originally narrated by gifted story-tellers, intended to provide meaning for the daily lives of their tribe members. Rules should be followed. Little girls shouldn't go wandering off by themselves in the woods. Mean stepsisters don't fit into the glass slipper the prince is looking to fill. Ultimately, these stories encouraged and taught me to anticipate happiness at some later time if I was just obedient and self-sacrificing enough. In hindsight, they also showed me the difference between male and female authority. Both Red Riding Hood and her grandmother are helpless victims who are saved only by the hunter-hero who rescues them from the male Big Bad Wolf. I, too, put my trust in some unworthy people over the years, at work and socially, who ended up lying and turning facts around in order to blame me for their own wrongdoing. The message is that both Red Riding Hood and I should have been wary of our choices in men, despite the harm that befell us. I believe this type of moral was a forerunner of the victim-shaming I later experienced.

It is 1995 and the evening of a leadership team year-end dinner with the company where I am the Director of Training and the head of the Sexual Harassment Investigation Committee.

Anthony, the president of the bottling company I work for, has a favorite restaurant. All our leadership dinners are held there in this densely populated section of Astoria, Queens. It amazes me how the valet parking works when there are never any empty spots on the crowded streets plus many double-parked cars and trucks on both the main and side streets. We try to carpool whenever possible to avoid having to wait for our cars late at night while the valets run all over town retrieving them.

Our customary dining space is in a semi-private room, tables arranged in a large square, with an even number of seats on each side. But what is the most amazing to me about this restaurant is the fact that we are never given menus. Anything we want is somehow produced seemingly out of thin air. I wonder if the kitchen staff runs around like the valet team, scrambling and negotiating for our dinner.

Consistently, I order Dover sole. But to tell you the truth, I could be given any white fish filet and would not know the difference. With the amount of alcohol freely flowing and the plates of appetizers, pastas, and homemade bread, the entrée I choose is wasted on me. In my entire life, I have never been treated to such an overabundance of delicious food accompanied by such individualized service. As soon as one person orders something different from the rest, platters of it are brought to the other sides of the table for sampling.

Then, too, there is the after-dinner grappa, a special kind of Italian wine with high alcohol content. On this one night, my colleagues on the leadership team tease me about being a wimp, never even trying it.

"You carpooled with Andre and will be sober by the time you get to your car," they cajole.

Boy, it does burn going down. But once I try it, the group turns to other delights, like ordering a huge assortment of pastries, desserts, espressos, and other after-dinner aperitifs.

Of all the men I work with during these seven years at this major beverage company, the CFO Andre is the only one who seems to grasp the concepts of using politically correct language, of advocating for training women in support and managerial roles, of understanding how the bottom line improves with every employee's success. He even presents me with an opportunity to travel to New Orleans with him to attend a convention for human resources professionals. Finding it difficult to connect with most of the men on that level of egalitarian consciousness, I accept another of his invitations to ride together to the leadership team dinner on this particular night.

The food, drinks, and camaraderie are highly festive this evening as we are nearing the Christmas holiday season, and the night goes on a little longer than I prefer. When we finally leave to go back and pick up my car, the conversation turns personal. Andre confides about his arranged marriage at a young age to a peasant girl from the little town where he grew up on the island of Trinidad. She was the daughter of a minister and had been groomed to serve. He tells me how they had come to America and built a home and family but how she never adapted or developed as an individual. He adds how lonely and misunderstood he feels. How ashamed he is having her for a partner, especially when the other members of the leadership team bring theirs to a corporate function. I listen to his tale with my counseling hat on, showing both empathy and encouragement for the possibility that their situation might be able to change in the future.

When he finishes, Andre asks about my marriage and divorce. "I know this is rather personal, but can you tell me what happened and how you came to make the decision to leave your marriage?"

I figure he is trustworthy because of his previous professionalism and because of his recent vulnerable confession.

Andre pulls the car over to the side of the road and listens intently, nodding, remaining actively connected without speaking. The space his silence offers me is huge and I keep spilling the story of my childhood. When I finish, he looks down at his hands and then quickly unzips his pants, grabbing my head from the back of my neck and pushing it down in between his legs. I am stunned. In the shock of that moment, three thoughts race through my mind:

I think I'm going to throw up.

How stupid can you be, Barbara, to always trust the wrong people?

How can I get away from here?

As I wrench my body upright and lean toward the passenger side door to leave, Andre grabs under my skirt and tears at my pantyhose, pulling them down. I jump out of the car and start to run with one leg of the hose hanging down around my knee and tears streaming down my face, retching up the glorious dinner as my insides twist. Feeling the grappa reburn my throat on its return trip through my mouth.

Andre backs up his car and drives slowly alongside me. Through the passenger side window, he first advises me to get back in the car. Then orders me. "Get back in the car, Barbara. You're making a scene."

I keep running. Fortunately, we are only four blocks from where my car is parked. As fast as I can find my keys with shaking hands, I get into my car, lock the door, then drive home. I sit behind the wheel feeling naked and dirty and ashamed of myself again. *Does it never end?* I scream into the empty space out loud.

With no one local to share what happened, the next morning I call a senior executive at the parent company, asking for her advice on how to handle my experience from the night before.

She does not hesitate to make a suggestion: "Write it all down exactly as it happened and put it in a sealed and dated envelope. Then hand deliver it to the personnel office and ask them to put it in your file until such time as you ask for it."

I feel a small sense of relief at having an action I can take immediately. She seems so confident, it sounds as though this is a tried and true way to keep the information on record. The only other thing I think of is to avoid facing Andre at any cost.

Imagine my surprise when a couple of weeks later, an ex-employee calls with a complaint about how the same CFO had tried to rape her. Now there are at least two of us and probably more in the wings. Because of my own experience with Andre, I know what to do: retrieve my file.

It is still amazing to me after all this time how the next parts of the drama unfold. The senior woman at the parent company denies ever having told me to write up what happened. The envelope I trusted to personnel has been opened and responses were planned for and already in motion. The personnel manager lies and says she saw me holding hands with the CFO, leading him on. One of the executives from the last leadership dinner says that after having grappa, I came up behind his chair and pressed my breasts into his back. Then the company attorney drops the big bomb: I am a divorcée. The company has multiple witnesses who can attest to me being sexually provocative and a liar. His final warning is that any further legal action I might take, the company would be compelled to expose the history with my father "to the world at large."

I meet with an attorney who specializes in cases of sexual harassment at work. While he says I have a fair court case, I need to be prepared for the worst.

"The company will make it look like you asked for this sexual mistreatment you got. They will call you a tease, a slut, a whore."

Overwhelmed thinking about public humiliation and the residual feelings of guilt from my childhood, I allow these men to silence me once again. My bravado and my voice are gone. Muted. Squelched. Victimizing the victim once more.

Only one person comes to my side. My executive assistant Pat explains what should have been obvious if I hadn't been so hurt and wounded.

"Why did the senior woman and the personnel manager both lie?" she asks, then answers the question. "To protect themselves. To save their jobs. To keep roofs over their heads and feed their families."

Pat adds without me asking, "And why did the men lie? Because they are all guilty of Andre's bad behavior and probably owe each other for covering for them some other time in the past. This is a macho, all-boys network that you mistakenly thought you broke into."

How is Pat, with only a high school education, so smart when I am her boss and so naïve?

Approximately three months later at our quarterly company-wide meeting, a right sizing of personnel is announced. That's the new buzzword to minimize the negativity that comes with an unexpected layoff of personnel. Positions will be consolidated and eliminated. Mine is one of them. I know my work performance is not in question. I have annual written reviews to validate that my work exceeds all expectations. The only way they can safely get rid of me is in a large group layoff.

We are all promised three more months' additional employment, good job recommendations, time off to interview, and the ability to collect unemployment insurance benefits thereafter. Now I am the one worried about keeping a roof over our heads and feeding my family.

I do land a job though before my current employment ends, with a $20,000 increase in pay. Not to mention, full tuition reimbursement toward earning a master's degree. Which I do.

It was only after I left my parents' home that I came to see how wrong I was about the future I'd allowed myself to dream about through these stories. Real adult life was more challenging than I imagined as a child.

My body and head had been fed and filled with misinformation, and I wasn't starting off with a strong foundation, built for me by two loving parents with my best interests at heart.

I believe that we are the sum total of all the decisions we have made in our lives. I haven't always made good ones. But that's for the next memoir.

Despite the behavior of caregivers in my life, there was and is something inside me, something inherent in who I am. An unwillingness to give up. A resilience that continues to push me forward every day. What doesn't kill you makes you stronger, they say. In my case, that is definitely true. I had to learn to grow and parent myself at a young age, sitting in the kindergarten closet on the first day of school. I am grateful that something inside me drove me to pursue the necessary work to heal in my adult years. A toughness even when

I was hurt and life looked its bleakest. To stretch myself and keep learning.

My arduous journey was successful in no small part because I became a self-help junkie. Included in my growth and development is forty years of psychotherapy, the est Training, Ira Progoff, Tony Robbins, Wayne Dyer, Marianne Williamson, Andrew Carnegie, and Woman Within to name a few.

My father's favorite saying was, "Children should be seen and not heard," which pushed me to want to be heard and visible. The closest I ever came to that level of communication at home was through books: encyclopedias, school textbooks, and pleasure reading. The words spoke to me. I heard voices as I read the letters on the page. The love of reading was a life preserver for me, keeping me above water. Later, in my corporate career, I taught women how to find their words and their voices. How to prevent sexual harassment and discrimination. Something I had not been able to do for myself up to that point. Finding the courage and confidence to help others ended up helping me as well. Knowing that I was the trainer, teacher, and mentor motivated me to learn everything I could on the subject. I earned certifications. I developed a course called NegoSHEation. I headed a corporate investigation committee. And with all that good work, I still managed to get stabbed in the back a few more times by trusting the wrong people.

My goal in telling the story of my upbringing was originally to stand in solidarity with another girl, another woman who thinks and feels she is all alone in the world with her secret. To shine a light and lead the way out of simply surviving and into healing. To normalize a difficult conversation that most people would sooner avoid. To bring that dark place into the spotlight. Now, however, I see that my purpose is to inspire conversations. To put secret topics out in the open so that there is less chance of them happening in the dark.

* * *

Two important people came into my life in the years that span beyond what this memoir covers, after the twenty-ninth year. The first one is Brett, my third child. The one who lived with me after I divorced his father. Who faced my job losses, multiple moves, and many substitute father figures with the men I was dating. Our relationship was essentially "you and me against the world." Through it all, he was a little boy with his nose constantly in a book. His imagination has led him to the business world within a creative niche. But what amazes me most about Brett is the loving husband and father he has become. He certainly did not see men doing that growing up. It makes me wonder again what parts of us are innate, nature vs. nurture.

The second important person to show up in my life is Geoff. My third, but what he refers to as my last, husband. His upbringing could have been taken right out of *Ozzie and Harriet*. His father worked to give his family stability and a middle-class life. Ham radios. Summer camp. College educations. His mother was the glue, the homemaker, raising three boys at the center of an extended family who were regulars in their home. The kids in the community they lived in slept over in each other's homes, ate meals at shared dinner tables, remained friends for life. Geoff still has friends he met in third grade. He is a problem solver who can listen and reflect, can talk things out first and find a solution that actually works for both of us. And when it doesn't work for both of us, he knows when I need the win more. He is a great family man, a fabulous lover and soulmate, a witness to my life without making me feel badly about any part of it, including my remaining triggers.

I used to think that love meant having someone to take care of me, who would give me the things I wanted just by wishing for them. I now know that love is sharing the responsibility. Growing individually and together. Supporting each other's goals and desires. Communicating. Speaking from the heart. Apologizing. Laughing. Holding each other through tears. Dancing. Partnering. Learning how to be unique individuals while living together. Love is choosing to stick with it and do it all over again and again.

I did see my father one more time even though I told him he couldn't count on my help or expect to see me again. Even though I walked out of his house without looking back. I visited him in hospice, six months after that final conversation.

The hospice nurse led Geoff and me down a quiet hallway to a room at the end. An old man laid on a bed there under several blankets with only his head showing. It was my father. But he looked so alien to me. My vision was suddenly drawn away by a hose running from the closet, spanning across the ceiling and leading to a machine he was connected to. The room was pulsating with the sound of this engine running.

"That's the morphine pump," the nurse explained when she caught me looking up and following the hose to its hidden source.

When I didn't respond, she must have misinterpreted my silence.

She put her hand on my shoulder. "Please don't worry about your father. We are making sure he is very comfortable. He's not feeling any pain."

Her words were punctuated by the sound of the pump operating, muffled as though I were swimming under water. I looked over at my father. He had lost considerable weight since the last time I saw him. His usual combover was not in place and the top of his head was bald with one very long side section hanging down. I had never seen my father unshaven. And without having shaved in a long time, he now had a thin scraggly gray beard, making him almost unrecognizable to me.

"It's okay to talk to him, to say goodbye," the nurse said, smiling over at me. Then she tipped her head to the side with her lips forming a frown and her eyes turned up like a Bassett hound's, sorrowful at the same time.

I was not about to tell this stranger anything about my relationship with my father. Geoff helped me out though by speaking at that moment.

"Jay. It's Barbara and Geoff. Just checking in on you." There was no reaction from my father. And I thought to myself, *Once again he has gotten someone to take care of him.* He does not have to be responsible even at the end. I left feeling grateful that I witnessed this last chapter of his life. Even with all the care he was being given, he was all alone.

A week later, I get a call from hospice. They are sorry to inform me that my father has passed away in his sleep. This call is followed up by one from the funeral home since I have been listed as next of kin. They need me to come down, sign some papers, and order death certificates. Then the bigger ask. Can I bring some clothing with me when I come in to dress him for the airplane trip back to New York? My parents had previously purchased burial plots there. Which means I have to go into his house and through his closet and dresser drawers to select an outfit for him to be buried in.

The front entrance to my parents' house still holds the combination lockbox to release the front door key. I remember the code and want to get in and out of there as quickly as possible.

In the first drawer I open, I find a gun and shudder. Including rifles on the floor and shelf his closet, there are eight more weapons. Why would a 93-year-old man living alone in a gated community with the protection of security guards need nine guns? As I continue searching, it is hard enough to go through his shirts, pants, ties, jackets, and shoes. I cannot touch his underwear. The thought of touching something intimate of his nauseates me. I start to gag, to dry heave, just thinking about what those undergarments touched. Where they have been. I shove the drawer closed. And I choose to leave him exposed. My father. Like he exposed me. Weeks later, when I speak at his funeral, I call him a complicated and flawed man. That is the nicest thing I can say without lying. A promise I make to myself with the freedom that comes from knowing he can never hurt me again. I will not lie, pretend, or acquiesce to someone else's expectations. No more secrets for me. I can finally speak the truth.

Acknowledgments

I tried to write this book two other times in my life. In my forties, I was accepted into a novel writing class at NYU by submitting three chapters and a book outline. While those chapters were apparently okay, the rest of my story was not.

The professor later told me, "Even *War and Peace* has some peace in it. No one will want to read this. It's too painful."

In my fifties, I joined a memoir writing class for seniors at my local public library. We were required to write three pages every week and make ten copies to distribute to the other participants for their feedback. At the end of the ten weeks, I felt like I had killed a tree, printing out those three hundred pages, and nothing much to show for it, except comments like "nice work."

What made this time different? Without the understanding of where I came from and how I got there, this story was very different.

Thank you to the late Cynthia Pascal and Carolynn Jarashow for their repair jobs. While they did not live to see their work completed, I hope their children do.

Thank you to Ellen Bass and Laura Davis, who wrote *The Courage to Heal: A Guide for Women Survivors of Child Sexual Abuse.* This was the first time I experienced the words of another incest survivor. It was powerful. And gratitude to Lindsay C. Gibson, PsyD, who wrote *Adult Children of Emotionally Immature Parents: How to Heal from Distant, Rejecting or Self-Involved Parents.* Her work gave me a whole new way of thinking about my parents and allowed me to let go of anger I was still holding toward them. Both researchers' insights acted as a comforting guide and an enlightening perspective along my journey.

Many thanks to One Billion Rising's anthem, "Break the Chain." Imagine taking an aerobic dance class and hearing a popular rock song with lyrics that include "no more rape, incest, or abuse" for the first time. I was not alone. So exhilarating.

To Suzanne Isaza (I never did find out her real last name) for introducing me to Incest AWARE and the community of survivors and advocates who work on education and prevention. Thank you.

Thank you to Jane Epstein of *Complicated Courage*, for recommending the Write Your Memoir in Six Months course. So proud to e-know you, Jane, and the brave work you are doing.

To Brooke Warner, mentor and publisher of She Writes Press, thank you for reading my work with such care, for asking the right questions in the right places, for getting me to fill in the blanks a reader would want to know. I am grateful to have had you as my midwife during this book birthing process.

To Linda Joy Myers, President of the National Association of Memoir Writers, thank you for helping me see the bigger picture, the universal story within my personal story.

Thank you, Cheryle Gail, of Brave Voices, who interviewed me on StoryCorps, where I tell my story for the Library of Congress and pay it forward interviewing other survivors.

To Geoff Wiland, thank you for being such an important part of my story. I have never known generosity like yours, of time and resources, of confidence and encouragement. The unconditional, ever replenished love that holds me in its safe embrace. Your love is like still having my two grandmothers here protecting me.

To Garry, thank you for getting me out of my dysfunctional family home and fathering our three incredible children. We have both grown up since those early days. I am happy that we've learned to express our love in healthy ways today.

FACING THE JAGUAR

* * *

I recently spoke to each of my adult children individually about my purpose in writing this memoir.

"I have no expectations that you will read it. Or that you will promote the book to your friends and colleagues. I did not write it for you. I wrote it to encourage others to speak about their family secrets too. To break the chain. Then, too, there probably will be things about my life that will surprise and upset you that you did not know about before."

My daughter Lindsay was first. "Why do I have to wait until the book comes out?" she asked. "Can't you send me the chapters as you write them? As you send them to your editor?"

Brett was second. "I don't think I can read a story about your pain. That will hurt me too." Then after hesitating, he added, "But I think I might have to read it so I can ask you questions while you're still around to answer them."

Adam's answer was a lot more direct and to the point. "Grandpa's dead. Does it make a difference?"

I am so proud of these three adults whom I had the privilege to watch grow into people I love and admire. And while I expect that I made plenty of mistakes in parenting them, I am sure that I was a good enough mother. I am especially grateful for the opportunity that was given me to end the cycle of abuse.

So yes. It does make a difference. To me for keeping a promise I made so long ago. And to others who are also the keepers of family secrets. We can't change what we can't speak about.

Trials like the ones I experienced in my life test us but don't define us. I am not what happened to me, good or bad. I am what I decided to do with those experiences. I have decided to tell.

Lastly, thank you dear reader for choosing to spend your time with me on this healing journey.

Resources

If you or someone you know is looking for a supportive community, check out the following organizations.

Incest Aware

An alliance of survivors, supporters and organizations on a mission to keep children safe from incest in the first place, secure safe methods of intervention, support survivors in recovery and end recidivism by transforming people who harm.

www.incestaware.org

RAINN

RAINN (Rape, Abuse & Incest National Network) is the nation's largest anti-sexual violence organization. RAINN created and operates the National Sexual Assault Hotline (800.656.HOPE, online. rainn.org and rainn.org/es) in partnership with more than 1,000 local sexual assault service providers across the country.

www.rainn.org

SAAN

At the Sexual Assault Advocacy Network (SAAN), our mission is to champion the rights and well-being of sexual assault survivors. We believe that every individual has the right to live free from the trauma of sexual violence.

www.saancommunity.org

Brave Voices

Brave Voices breaks the cycle of silence that perpetuates childhood sexual abuse. Every adult contributes to the reduction of harm by speaking up. Use your voice to normalize the conversation.

www.bravevoices.org

About the Author

Photo credit: Elise Campbell Photography

Babs Walters is a speaker, advocate, and author as well as a survivor of domestic violence and childhood sexual abuse. She brings difficult subjects to the surface through the power of storytelling.

With a master's in counseling human relations, Walters developed creative, healing, journal-writing workshops for women in alcohol and drug recovery. During her corporate career, she led workshops on preventing sexual harassment and continues to teach women to raise their voices today.

Babs lives in Southeast Florida where she teaches Jazzercise and enjoys time with family. Learn more at BabsWalters.com.

Looking for your next great read?

We can help!

Visit www.shewritespress.com/next-read
or scan the QR code below for a list
of our recommended titles.

She Writes Press is an award-winning
independent publishing company founded to
serve women writers everywhere.